Anin

Horace G. Richards

Alpha Editions

This edition published in 2020

ISBN : 9789354018572

Design and Setting By
Alpha Editions
email - alphaedis@gmail.com

ANIMALS *of the* SEASHORE

by

HORACE G. RICHARDS

RESEARCH ASSOCIATE, NEW JERSEY STATE MUSEUM

BOSTON

BRUCE HUMPHRIES, INC.

PUBLISHERS

To My Parents

PREFACE

Every year thousands of vacationists visit the summer resorts of the New Jersey coast. The population of such resorts as Atlantic City, Cape May, Wildwood, and Beach Haven is doubled many times when the warm summer months send throngs of Philadelphians, New Yorkers, as well as residents of more distant places, to the seashore to enjoy the cool breezes and the salt water bathing.

Rivaling New Jersey's beaches, Long Island has its Rockaway, Jones Beach and many other resorts from the popular Coney Island to the ultra-fashionable Southampton Beach.

South of New Jersey, we find Rehoboth Beach, Delaware, Ocean City, Maryland, Virginia Beach, Virginia, and scores of smaller resorts that in their turn draw countless summer visitors from the inland cities.

Many of these vacationsts like to walk along the beach and look with curiosity upon the strange forms of animal life that can be found in the tide pools, the mud flats or washed on the sandy shores. While these sea shells, corals, and the like may not be as beautiful or colorful as those found on the more tropical beaches, they also have much beauty and fascination and often have peculiar stories to tell. It is of these sea animals, found along our Middle Atlantic Coast, that this guide book attempts to treat.

In addition to being a guide for the summer visitor to the seashore, it is hoped that this book will be used by students in schools and colleges and that it will encourage them to try to learn something more of the strange creatures that live between the tides or beneath the waters of the ocean.

No pretense is made at a complete catalogue of the invertebrate animals of the East Coast, or even those of the State of New Jersey. An attempt has been made, however, to discuss and illustrate all of the common and many of the rarer species that would be found by the casual collector along the coast of New Jersey and its neighboring states. While many of the records are specifically from New Jersey, the same animals would in most cases be found in similar situations between Cape Cod and Cape Hatteras. Thus it is hoped that the book also will serve as a guide to the study of the sea animals found along the seashore between Southern New England and the Carolinas.

The author began collecting and studying the sea animals of the New Jersey coast in 1927 while a student at the University of Pennsylvania, and for a while was associated with Professor A. E. Parr in a survey of this coast conducted by the United States Bureaus of Fisheries.

The identifications of many of the species have been verified by specialists in the respective branches of zoology. In addition to checking the identification, certain of these specialists have critically read the manuscript of the chapters or sections on the particular group of animals in which they are most interested. For such splendid cooperation the author is indebted to the following:-

Dr. O. E. Nelsen, University of Pennsylvania (Coelenterata)

Mr. A. H. Clark, United States National Museum (Echinoderms)

Dr. R. S. Osburn, Ohio State University (Bryozoa)

Dr. J. P. Moore, University of Pennsylvania (Worms)

Dr. A. Treadwell, Vassar College (Worms)

Mr. E. G. Vanatta, Academy of Natural Sciences (Mollusks)

Dr. Waldo L. Schmitt, United States National Museum (Crustacea)

Dr. Mary J. Rathbun, United States National Museum (Decopoda)

Mr. Clarence Shoemaker, United States National Museum (Amphipoda)

Mr. J. O. Maloney, United States National Museum (Isopoda)

Dr. H. A. Pilsbry, Academy of Natural Sciences (Cirripedia)

Dr. Willard G. Van Name, American Museum of Natural History (Tunicates)

While many of the identifications have been checked by these specialists, it has not been possible to have this done in all cases, so the author assumes the responsibility for the identifications used in this book.

Many of the illustrations are original; others have been borrowed from various sources. The author is especially indebted to the New York Zoological Society, the New Jersey State Museum and the Academy of Natural Sciences of Philadelphia for the loan of certain cuts.

Photographs of published and unpublished illustrations were supplied by the United States National Museum, the American Museum of Natural History, the Connecticut Geological and Natural History Survey (through Dr. W. R. Coe), the Museum of Zoology, Copenhagen, Denmark (through

O. T. Mortensen), Dr. R. C. Osburn, Dr. R. S. Bassler, Dr. W. G. Van Name, and Mr. L. C. Brownell.

Permission to copy certain published illustrations, either by photographing or drawing, has kindly been granted by the United States Bureau of Fisheries, the Carnegie Institution of Washington and the Museum of Comparative Zoology of Harvard University.

The drawings of Plates 2, 3, 11, 13, Fig. 2, as well as the map were made by Mr. Walter Ziomek of the New Jersey State Museum and those of Figs 5, 8, 9 and 10, by Mr. John Boczek.

Unfortunately, space will not permit the acknowledgment of all who have aided in the preparation of the book—the collecting and the study of the material as well as the task of preparing the manuscript and the plates for publication.

CONTENTS

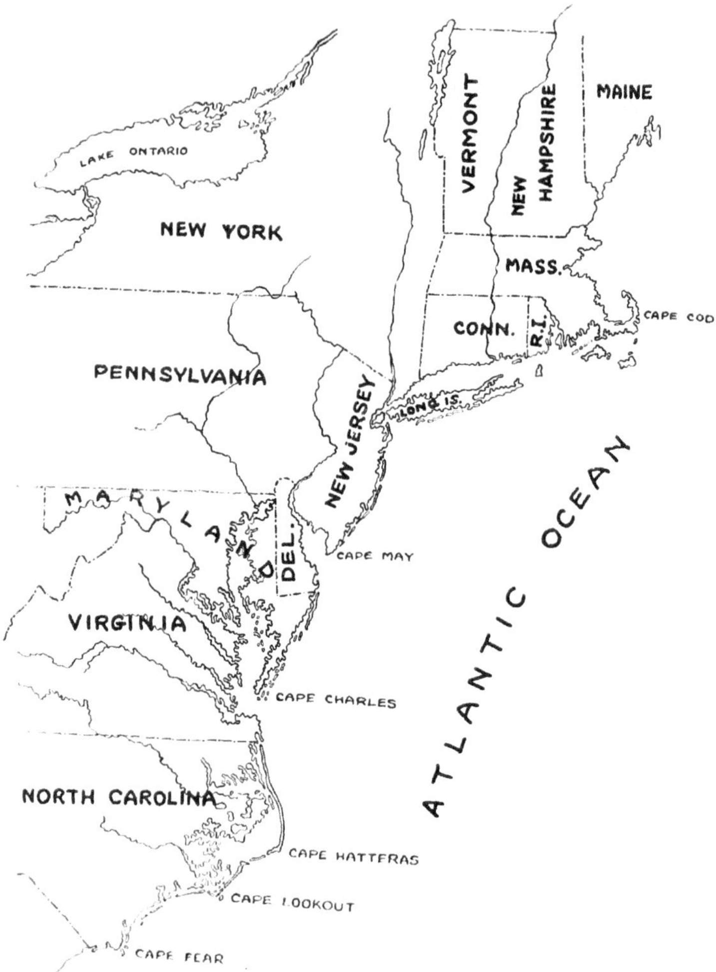
LAKE ONTARIO
NEW YORK
VERMONT
NEW HAMPSHIRE
MAINE
MASS.
CONN.
R.I.
CAPE COD
PENNSYLVANIA
NEW JERSEY
LONG IS.
MARYLAND
DEL.
CAPE MAY
ATLANTIC OCEAN
VIRGINIA
CAPE CHARLES
NORTH CAROLINA
CAPE HATTERAS
CAPE LOOKOUT
CAPE FEAR

CHAPTER ONE

THE OCEAN AND ITS INHABITANTS

Ever since the earliest times the ocean has held a fascination for man. At first it was worshipped as a superhuman power, or personified as a god such as the Roman Neptune or the Greek Poseidon. Later man strove to conquer its mysteries and to learn something concerning its great extent, its depth and also the animals and plants that lived beneath its surface.

By the beginning of the Christian era there had been numerous voyages of discovery and man had become more acquainted with some of the mysteries of the sea. Many strange animals had been collected from various parts of the ocean. About this time the Roman naturalist, Pliny the Elder, compiled a natural history in which he listed 176 animals from the ocean. He must have been rather pleased with his work, for he remarked: "By Hercules, there exists nothing in the sea and in the ocean, vast as they are, that is unknown to us, and, a truly marvelous fact, it is with these things that nature has concealed in the deep that we are best acquainted."

Today we are not quite so sure that we know all the animals of the ocean. Every expedition to remote parts of the world brings back scores of new species of sea animals and even explorations in waters nearer home frequently bring to light specimens either new to science or not hitherto reported in this part of the world.

Sea animals, like the rest of the animal kingdom, are divided into two main groups, vertebrates and invertebrates. The vertebrates include those animals that possess a backbone. In the sea this group is represented by the fishes, whales, porpoises and a few lesser known animals. The other group, the invertebrates, includes the more primitive forms of animal life. Although many species are very small, the invertebrates comprise the great majority of the inhabitants of the sea. These creatures, such as the jelly-fish, starfish, crabs, the inhabitants of sea shells and the like, make up the most conspicuous feature of the animal life of the seashore. Even the most casual visitor to the seacoast cannot help but observe a few of the invertebrate animals of the region, even if it be only on the dining room table. Moreover, a great many visitors to the shore make collections of the various shells, crabs, or other specimens that they find washed upon the beach. It is with these invertebrate animals that we shall be concerned in this book.

Various systems of classification of the invertebrate animals have been proposed. According to the arrangement used here there are ten main divisions or phyla, each one of which is discussed in a separate chapter with the exception of the phylum Arthropoda which is discussed in three chapters, one dealing with the Crustacea (Crabs, Shrimp, etc.), another with the Arachnoidea (Spiders, King Crabs, etc.) and the third with the Insecta (Insects). The various phyla are in turn divided into smaller groups—classes, orders and families. Only a few of the more important subdivisions are outlined in this book since their description would require the use of too many technical terms.

A family is composed of a number of different animals that are all closely related. Each kind of animal has two names—first a genus name which always comes first and begins with a capital letter; this is followed by a species name which always begins with a small letter even if it is named for a person or place. Closely related animals have the same genus name but always different species names. In a few cases there is a third or variety name which follows the species name, but for most animals two names are sufficient.

The name of the animal is always followed by the name of the man who first described it. For instance, *Asterias forbesi* Desor is the common starfish and was first described by Desor in 1848 and was named in the honor of Forbes. *Asterias tenera* Stimpson is a related starfish that was described by Stimpson. The fact that they have the same genus name shows that they are closely related.

CHAPTER TWO

SEA ANIMALS OF THE ATLANTIC COAST

The marine animals of the Atlantic coast of North America can be classified roughly speaking by the zones or provinces in which they live. Obviously these zones are not separated from each other by sharp lines, but nature has created a great many factors that play a part in the distribution of sea animals and no form of animal or plant life will conform to arbitrary man-made laws or boundaries. Certain of these zones are better differentiated than others. So, while this grouping of animals into regions is arbitrary and not always accurate, it does serve as a convenience and is often of considerable help to both the amateur collector and the student of marine life.

Perhaps the most important boundary is Cape Cod. Any visitor to the region will perceive the considerable difference in ocean temperature north and south of the cape. It has long been recognized that the waters around Cape Cod were the meeting place of two faunas, the Acadian from the north and the Virginian from the south. It was once pointed out that there is a greater difference between the marine algae (seaweeds) of Massachusetts Bay and Buzzards Bay which are just a few miles apart, the former north of Cape Cod and the latter south of it, than there is between the flora of Massachusetts Bay and the Bay of Fundy, or between those of

Nantucket and Norfolk. The same thing, perhaps in a lesser degree, is true of the marine animals. The most important reason for this fact is the presence of the cold Labrador Current north of Cape Cod and the warm Gulf Stream that flows south of the cape.

Other factors also play a part. For instance, Cape Cod itself acts as a barrier and helps keep distinct the animals north and south of that cape. Again, the rocky coast of New England is very different from the sandy beaches of the south shore of Long Island and from New Jersey southward. This variation in habitat accounts for some of the differences in the marine life of the two regions.

Proceeding southward the next important boundary line is reached at Cape Hatteras and here again we note a marked change in the fauna. As at Cape Cod, there is a noticeable difference in the water temperature north and south of Hatteras, although here the change is more gradual. The Gulf Stream, which is fairly close to the shore from Florida north to Hatteras, is deflected out to sea at this point and proceeds northward a greater distance from shore. The warmer waters south of Cape Hatteras allow the growth of coral reefs and thereby afford a habitat for sea animals not known north of that cape.

There is somewhat of a boundary at the southern part of Florida and many species are restricted to the perpetually warm seas of the Florida Keys, the Bahamas and the West Indies. It is in these tropical waters that one finds the greatest variety and abundance and beauty of marine life. The many colored shells are rivalled by the brillance of the corals, sea fans, sponges and other inhabitants of the tropical sea.

The region north of Cape Cod is sometimes divided into two zones with a boundary at the Gulf of St. Lawrence. This boundary, like that of southern Florida, is not well defined and the transition between the two is more gradual.

The following zones may thus be recognized:

Arctic	Arctic Seas to the Gulf of St. Lawrence
Acadian	Gulf of St. Lawrence to Cape Cod
Virginian	Cape Cod to Cape Hatteras
Carolinian	Cape Hatteras to Florida
Caribbean	Florida Keys, West Indies, etc.

The region to be treated in this book lies in the Virginian Zone—between Cape Cod and Cape Hatteras. Although most of the animals described and illustrated were actually obtained from the coast of New Jersey, practically the same fauna would be found along the entire coast between the two above mentioned capes.

Near Cape Cod, however, a large number of species from the Acadian Zone lap over into the region south of Cape Cod. In addition, many rock dwelling forms extend their range as far south as Long Island, the southern limit of the rocky coastline. Because of this overlapping of faunas, the region in the vicinity of the Marine Biological Laboratory at Woods Hole, Massachusetts has a rather large fauna composed of both northern and southern elements.

Again, at and near Hatteras we find a mingling of the faunas, and many Carolinian or Caribbean species extend some distance north of that cape.

As we have seen, this zoning is very arbitrary and the animals will not stay within their "proper" zones. This point is brought out in the following chapters when numerous species are recorded for the first time in New Jersey far north or south of their known distribution.

Furthermore, many animals, common in shallow water along the northeastern coast, extend south in deeper water where the temperature is lower. Certain echinoderms and mollusks, which are common in shallow water along the coast of Maine and Northern New England, extend their range as far south as Cape Hatteras in water of considerable depth. Among these may be mentioned the Green Sea Urchin (*Strongylocentrotus drobachiensis*), the Bloody Starfish (*Henricia sanguinolenta*) and the Sea Scallop (*Pecten grandis*).

In addition, certain northern animals extend their ranges southward during the colder months of the winter; conversely numerous southern animals migrate north of their normal range in the warmest parts of the summer.

There are so many factors that combine to determine the distribution of marine animals that it is very difficult to map even approximate zones. Nevertheless, the above mentioned zones have certain characteristic species and are used as a matter of convenience.

Chapter Three

COLLECTING ALONG THE NEW JERSEY COAST

The shore-line of New Jersey from Bay Head to Cape May is made up of coastal islands, separated from each other and from the mainland by bays and inlets. These islands vary in width from a few hundred yards to more than a mile. Above Bay Head there are numerous inlets but the mainland extends down to the ocean. On the bay side of these islands is the salt marsh.

This same description, with slight modifications, would hold true for the entire Virginian Zone, from the South Shore of Long Island to Cape Hatteras, North Carolina.

* * *

Seashore animals are usually particular about their place of living; some prefer the mud flats of the harbors and bays while others prefer a sandy association; still others require a rocky situation. Many of these animals also have distinct preferences as to the depth of water. Some are always found between the tides while others prefer the shallow water a short distance off shore. Then there are the deep sea dwellers—those animals that live in the extreme depths of the ocean and which seldom or never are found near shore.

The usual collector is interested in those animals which he can obtain most readily, namely the forms of the littoral or intertidal zone, or those of the shallow sea which are frequently cast upon the beach by the waves.

Perhaps the best places to obtain a large number of different kinds of sea animals are tidal mud flats such as occur along the various bays, harbors and inland waterways of the region. The soft nature of the mud makes it easy for many species to burrow down and build their homes. In addition, the mud flats are usually protected from the action of the waves. It is in such associations that one finds various species of worms, sea cucumbers, and many mud-boring mollusks such as both the Hard Shell (*Venus mercenaria*) and Soft Shell (*Mya arenaria*) Clam, the Razor Clam (*Ensis directus*), the Large Angel Wings (*Pholas costata*).

On the surface of these flats can usually be seen thousands of Mud Snails (*Nassa obsoleta*) and Fiddler Crabs (*Uca pugnax*).

A sandy beach is not a good place to look for living sea animals. It is usually difficult for these animals to burrow into the hard sand and they would consequently be exposed to the force of the waves. Some animals, however, have adapted themselves to this type of association and can be looked for on sandy beaches. Some worms burrow in the sand between tides while a few species actually construct more or less permanent tubes out of the sand grains (*Sabellaria vulgaris*, *Cistenides gouldii*, etc.).

The Sand Crab or Ghost Crab (*Ocypoda albicans*) can frequently be seen scurrying over the beach and disappearing into its hole near or above high water mark. The Sand Bug or Hippa (*Emerita talpoida*) and the Lady Crab (*Ovalipes ocellatus*) burrow into the sand close to low water mark. Among the mollusks the Surf Clam (*Mactra solidissima*), the Moon Snail (*Polinices duplicatus*) and the tiny Wedge Clam (*Donax fossor*) often live along sandy beaches.

Many animals of the shallow sea zone, or the off shore communities, are often found on the beach where they have been carried by the waves. If one walks along one of the New Jersey beaches after a severe storm, he is apt to find a great variety of strange sea animals that have been washed either living or dead upon the beach.

After one storm the beach may be strewn with thousands of Red Sponges (*Microciona prolifera*) carried from the oyster grounds of Delaware Bay. After another storm one may find instead a great many tropical species carried from the Gulf Stream which lies about 100 miles off shore. The Portuguese Man of War (*Physalia pelagica*), the Gulf Weed Crab (*Planes minutus*), and other unusual specimens are among the rarer visitors to the New Jersey coast.

New England is noted for its "stern and rock-bound coast," New Jersey for its sandy beaches. Certain species of sea animals are usually found associated with rocks and would not be expected along the sandy coast of New Jersey. However, in recent years, rock jetties and breakwaters have been built at a number of places along the coast of that state and thus homes are provided for some of these rock-loving species. Among the New England species that are seldom found in New Jersey waters except on the "Rock Piles" are the Periwinkles (*Littorina litorea, L. rudis* and *L. palliata*) and the Rock Barnacle (*Balanus balanoides*).

The woodwork of wharves and piling are often covered with marine life. Sponges, hydroids, bryozoa, sea anemones, sea squirts, mussels and Ivory-Barnacles, together with a dense growth of algae, almost completely cover many such wooden structures. Destructive species such as the Ship Worm (*Teredo navalis*), the boring isopod (*Limnoria lignorum*) are also found wherever there is unprotected wood.

The species of the salt marsh are usually very limited in number. The water is brackish, being diluted with fresh water, and is harmful to many species. Moreover, parts of the marshes are entirely exposed above the water for certain periods of time. The animals of the salt marsh must be able to withstand these changing conditions. Among the species most characteristic of the New Jersey salt marshes are the Horse Mussel (*Modiolus demissus*), the Fiddler Crabs (*Uca pugnax, U. pugilator, U. minax*), the Salt Marsh Periwinkle (*Littorina irrorata*) and the Coffee Snail (*Melampus linetaus*).

To obtain the animals of the shallow sea zone it is most desirable to obtain a boat. A small dredge or even a bucket or shrimp net can be dragged behind a row boat. In this way it is possible to obtain a small idea of some of the inhabitants of the shallow water close to shore especially in the bays and harbors.

As one goes farther out to sea, the depth of the water increases and with it the difficulty of obtaining specimens from the bottom of the sea. A larger boat and more elaborate equipment are necessary for water deeper than a few fathoms.

As we have seen, many of these off shore animals are frequently uprooted from their homes at the bottom of the sea and carried to the beach. The easiest way to collect some of these off shore animals is to walk leisurely along one of the beaches after a severe storm.

Obviously the animals of the greatest depths are seldom or never carried to the beaches. It is only those that live within a reasonable distance off shore and at a reasonable depth that are even occasionally found along the beach. For that reason we will consider here, with a few exceptions, only those species that live within about twenty-five miles of the shore and in water of twenty-five fathoms (150 feet) or less in depth.

Chapter Four

FOSSIL SHELLS OF THE NEW JERSEY BEACHES

It is well known that the oceans have not always been in exactly the same places that they are today. We know that at certain times in the history of the earth the seas were higher and covered certain parts of what is now land. Variations in the amount of water in the sea together with movements of the land have brought about these various changes in the position of the oceans.

We find evidence for these ancient seas in the fossil remains of sea animals—vertebrate and invertebrate—that are found far from the present seashore, even on the tops of mountains. Fossils are defined as "remains or traces of animals or plants that lived in a period earlier than the present." They may be petrified remains, or they may be unaltered, consisting of the hard parts of the original animal, such as bones or shells. Ordinarily fossil sea animals are easily recognized because they are different from living species and because they are often found far from salt water.

Fossil shells are often found washed up on the sea beaches where they have been carried from some nearby deposits on land or perhaps from some deposit at the bottom of the sea. Many of these shells are unaltered, and are difficult or impossible to distinguish from recent shells. In many cases, the species are extinct and are not to be found living anywhere in present seas. Such species are common along parts of Chesapeake Bay and at certain places along the coast of North and South Carolina.

Fossil shells are frequently found on the New Jersey beaches, but they are almost always those of species still living in the ocean. While they cannot always be spotted with certainty, they can often be recognized by their black color and worn character.

While most of these fossil shells belong to species still living in the sea, there are a few that are not living in the waters of New Jersey today. Some of these live in warmer seas farther south between Cape Hatteras and Florida. These are thought to have lived perhaps 100,000 years ago during the last interglacial stage, just before the last great ice sheets came down from the north. The seas were probably warmer then than at present and it would have been possible for these warm water animals to have lived as far north as New Jersey. The deposit containing these fossils is known as the Cape May formation.

During interglacial time there was more water in the sea than at present because there was less ice on the earth; the melting of the polar glaciers had poured an extra quantity of water into the sea causing it to submerge parts of the present land. The advance of the ice in (Wisconsin) glacial time caused sea level to fall.

In a few places along the New Jersey coast fossils from this interglacial sea are found in gravel, sand or clay above present sea level. However, better fossils are obtained below the surface in well borings or dredgings.

At certain places along the New Jersey coast, especially on the coastal islands, real estate developments have been created by pumping sand upon the salt marshes by means of hydraulic dredging from 30 to 50 feet below the bottom of the thoroughfares or channels back of the coastal islands. In the sand thus pumped to the surface are often shells and other remains of sea animals. These are probably from the Cape May formation which underlies these coastal islands, and which, as we have just seen, was deposited during the last interglacial stage. Many of the species now live only in more southern waters and are the same as those frequently found washed up on the beach. Two Mile Beach, south of Wildwood, is the best place to collect these fossil shells. Other similar hydraulic fills are found all along the New Jersey coast, as well as at a few places on the "Del-Mar-Va Peninsula."

Some of the commoner of these warm water fossils are listed in the chapters on mollusks. The following is the complete list of the Pleistocene shells of New Jersey which at present are restricted to the warmer seas south of that state: *Terebra concava*, *T. dislocata*, *Fulgur perversum*, *Polinices lactea*, *Sinum perspectivum*, *Thais floridana*, *Fissurella alternata*, *Mangelia stellata*, *Cantharus cancellaria*, *Arca ponderosa*, *Transenella stimpsoni*, *Rangia cuneata*, *Odostomia impressa* var. *granitina*, *Chione cribaria*. In addition these fossil deposits contain many species still living in the region.

A few species of fossil shells from the New Jersey beaches are known alive only from the seas north of New Jersey and thus indicate a former colder temperature. It is probable that these shells lived in the sea during Glacial times, perhaps 25,000 years ago when the climate was colder than it is today because immense ice sheets covered the northern parts of earth.

There was less water in the sea than at present because immense quantities of water were locked up in the land ice. The shore line of New Jersey consequently extended far beyond its present position. For instance, the site of Atlantic City would have been some 75 miles from the sea! Fossils laid down in this glacial sea would have been deposited far from the present shore line and would consequently seldom be found on the beach except when they were carried by unusually heavy seas.

The following species, at present only living north of New Jersey, probably lived in this glacial sea: *Buccinum undatum, Neptunea decemcostata* and *Colus gracilis*. *Neptunea stonei*, an extinct gastropod of northern affinities, probably also is a shell of this glacial sea. All these species are very rare on the New Jersey beaches.

CHAPTER FIVE

PORIFERA
(The Sponges)

Sponges at one time were regarded as plants. When, at last, their animal nature was discovered, their exact relationship and position in the animal kingdom was not clear. For a while they were thought to be large colonies or masses of unicellular, microscopic animals. Finally, from a study of their life history, it was concluded that they were individual multicellular animals. Although there are a great many microscopic animals made up of a single cell (Protozoa), the sponges are usually regarded as the simplest group of multicellular animals (Metazoa).

The sponge with which everyone is familiar, the commercial Bath Sponge, is really only the dried skeleton of the original living animal. When these large sponges are seen alive in their native environment, such as off the coast of Florida, they can be seen to be covered with a thin gelatinous layer of skin. After the sponges are obtained from their home at the bottom of the sea, they are dried and in this way the fleshy skin is removed.

The greatest variety of sponges of the east coast of North America is found off Florida, the Bahamas and the West Indies. Visitors to Tarpon Springs, Florida, or to Nassau, Bahamas, often visit the sponge boats to see the interesting diving equipment and the unusual animals found at the bottom of the sea associated with the sponges. Great quantities of sponges can usually be seen drying on the wharves.

Although the large commercial sponges are found only in warm seas, there are a number of varieties that are found all along the east coast of the United States. While these are mostly small and of no commercial value, some are very beautiful.

A few sponges have rather peculiar habits. The Red Sponge (*Microciona prolifera*) is often found growing on the back of Spider Crabs which use the sponge as a camouflage. The Sulphur Sponge (*Cliona celata*) bores into shells of oysters, clams and other bivalves, and finally succeeds in killing the bivalve.

Sponges have no regular mouths. Their bodies contain a great number of small canals which finally open again to the outside through larger openings or oscula. These oscula are fairly conspicuous in the ordinary Bath Sponge. Sea water is constantly flowing through these canals, entering the sponge through the small pores and leaving it through the larger oscula. As this steady stream of water is passing through the sponge, the small microscopic plants and animals in the water are removed by the sponge and utilized as food.

The skeletal framework of sponges is composed of a great many small fibers of a horny, calcareous or silicious substance. These fibers are known as spicules, and are very important in the classification of the various species of sponges.

Cliona celata Grant (Sulphur Sponge, Boring Sponge, Yellow Coral, "Punk")
(*Cliona sulphurea Desor*)

PLATE I. Fig. 1, 4

The Boring Sponge is fairly common in New Jersey waters, especially in the oyster grounds in Delaware Bay, where it bores into the oyster shells. This sponge usually consists of small, yellow, wart-like protuberances which project about one-eighth of an inch above the shell. However, at times it grows out of the shell which it has excavated and assumes a massive form, sometimes as much as three feet square. This massive form of the sponge is known to the fishermen as "Yellow Coral" or "Punk" and is frequently associated with good fishing grounds. It is especially abundant in Delaware Bay near "Old Bare Shoal," off the mouth of Mispillion River, Delaware, in Maurice River Cove on the New Jersey side of the bay and in Ludlam's Bay near Sea Isle City, New Jersey. It is present, but less conspicuous in other parts of the New Jersey coastal waters. It is rarely found in the open ocean.

Many shells, especially the Oyster and Clam (*Venus*), are cast up on the beach riddled with small holes, showing the work of this sponge.

Chalina arbuscula Verrill (Dead Man's Fingers)

PLATE I. Fig. 2

This branched or finger-like sponge lives in

PLATE I

1. **Cliona celata** Grant
2. **Chalina arbuscula** Verrill
3. **Microciona prolifera** Verrill
4. Shell bored by **Cliona celata** Grant

1

2

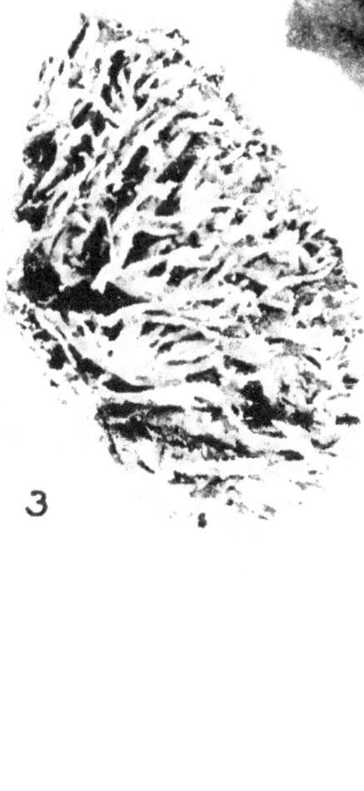

3

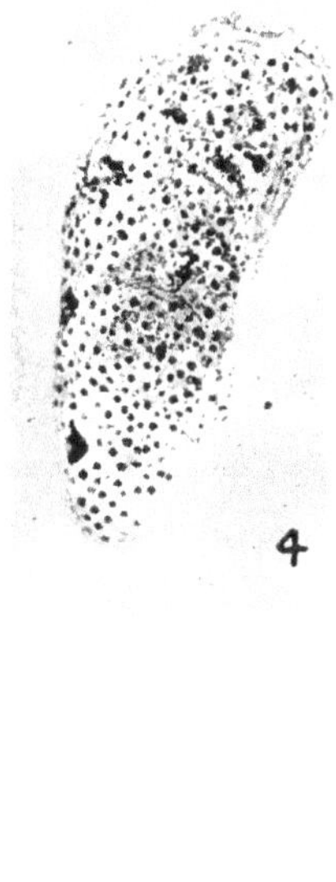

4

water about fifty feet deep some ten miles off the New Jersey coast. It is buff or grayish when alive but as it dries it turns a yellowish color. Dried specimens are occasionally found washed up on the New Jersey beaches particularly in the northern part of the state (Sandy Hook to Barnegat).

This sponge occurs in shallow water from Cape Cod to Cape Hatteras. A closely related species, *Chalina oculata* occurs off the coast of northern New England.

Microciona prolifera Verrill (Red Sponge)

PLATE I. Fig. 3

This is the most common of the New Jersey sponges. When young, it forms thin bright red incrustations on shells; when fully grown, it rises in irregular slender branches as much as six inches high. It is very abundant on the oyster shells in Maurice River Cove in Delaware Bay, Ludlam's Bay, Great Egg Harbor, Barnegat Bay and many other parts of the Inland Coastal Waterways of New Jersey. It is seldom found in the open ocean or washed up on the ocean beaches.

In the spring, after the breaking up of the ice, many sponges are dislodged from their shell and washed upon the beaches of Delaware Bay. The beaches at Cape May Point in early April are frequently covered with great masses of this red sponge which turns brown as it dries. The same occurrence is noted after severe storms, for instance after the "Northeaster" of April 12, 1928. It frequently grows on the back of spider crabs

(*Libinia*). At certain times this sponge is said to be poisonous.

Found from New England to the Carolinas.

Suberites compacta Verrill

An irregular elongate sponge, bright yellow in color, occasionally found attached to shells or stranded on the beach. Known from Maine to Virginia but rare in New Jersey.

Chapter Six

COELENTERATA

1. HYDROZOA Hydroids and small jellyfish
2. SCYPHOZOA Larger jellyfish
3. ACTINOZOA Sea Anemones and Corals

HYDROZOA

Hydroids at first glance resemble plants rather than animals for they appear to have a stem, root, branches and even flowers. In fact, they are very often collected and preserved as sea-weeds. Nevertheless, they are really animals, or more strictly speaking, groups or colonies of associated animals. A true hydroid colony is made up of two, or in some cases three, kinds of individuals or polyps, each performing different functions for the benefit of the entire colony. Some individuals have mouths and tentacles and obtain the food for the colony; these are the nutritive polyps. Other individuals serve a reproductive function and produce the young of the next generation. Some species possess a third type of individual, serving a protective function. These may be armed with thousands of small stinging cells which serve the double purpose of protecting the colony from enemies and in paralyzing the prey which is to be used as food.

Many of the species of Hydrozoa pass through what is known as Alternation of Generations; in other words, they have two distinct forms, (1) the hydroid stage, briefly described above and (2) the medusa or jellyfish stage. As we have just seen, this plant-like hydroid possesses reproductive polyps; by a form of budding these polyps produce minute jellyfish. In many species these break loose from the colony and become free-swimming hydromedusae. Although very minute when liberated, they may attain a size of an inch or so at maturity. In some species they always remain very minute and attached to the hydroid stalk.

When the medusa is mature, it produces eggs which soon develop into minute free-swimming organisms known as planuae. Soon, however, these planulae settle down and attach themselves to some object and grow, plant-like, into a hydroid. Thus the cycle is completed. The animal has passed through an alternation of two generations (1) the hydroid stage which reproduces by plant-like budding (asexually) to form (2) the medusa stage which in turn reproduces by eggs (sexually) to again form the hydroid.

These two forms, hydroid and medusa, are totally different in appearance and one would never suspect that they belonged to the same species. In fact, early naturalists did not realize this and gave different names to the two stages.

Not all Hydrozoa pass through the same life history. Some species have only a hydroid stage, while others have only a medusa. One group (Siphonophora) consists of large free-floating communities. The Portuguese Man of War (*Physalia pelagica*) is the best known example of this group. (see page 59)

Most of the hydroids are very small and are easily overlooked by the casual collector. The species are usually very difficult to determine and the identifications are based upon the size, shape and position of the reproductive polyps (gonosomes) and upon the structure of the nutritive polyp or hydranth. Some hydranths are uncovered (Tubularidae) while most are protected by a horny receptacle or hydrotheca.

Hydroids are usually attached to some solid object by a root-like structure (hydrorhiza), although a few float freely on the surface of the sea. From this root arises the main stalk, which is usually branched and from these branches hang the various polyps.

The medusa stage resembles a tiny umbrella. At the lower part of the handle (manubrium) is the mouth which opens into various canals. A membraneous velum or veil usually projects inward from the rim of the umbrella.

The average collector along the New Jersey coast will find only three conspicuous hydroids—*Tubularia crocea* and *Hydractinia echinata* and *Thuiaria argentea*. Most of the other species are small and in order to identify them it is necessary to make a careful study of their structure with a fairly high powered microscope. The student especially interested in the Hydrozoa will find them adequately treated in the references cited in the bibliography. For the benefit of the more casual student, condensed descriptions of some of the New Jersey forms are given here. In writing these descriptions free use has been made of the sources cited in the bibliography.

Tubularian Hydroids

Hydroids with naked hydranths, that is, without any protective cups (hydrothecae).

This pinkish covering is found on shells and occasionally on pebbles throughout the entire coastal waters of New Jersey, as well as along the New England coast. The shells covered by *Hydractinia* are frequently inhabited by Hermit Crabs (*Parugus*).

Under the microscope or fairly powerful lens the rather complicated organization of this colony can be observed. There is a root-like net work covering the surface of the shell; from this covering various polyps or individuals of the colony arise.

Hydractinia echinata Fleming

Fig. 1

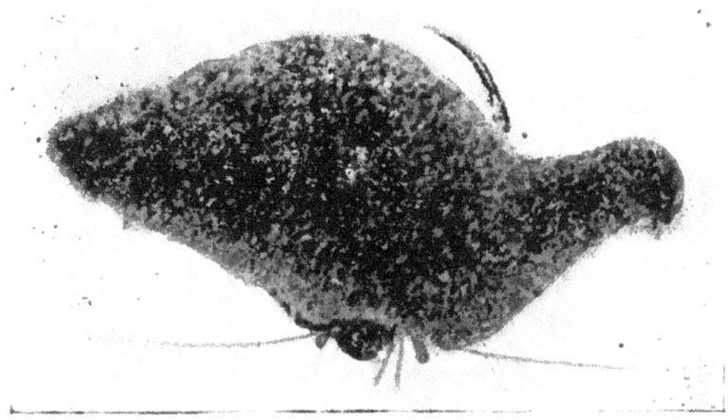

Hydractinia echinata Fleming

There are three types of polyp: one for feeding, one for reproduction and a third type for protection, armed with stinging cells or nematocysts.

The peculiar association between the *Hydractinia* and the Hermit Crab in the shell is known as commensalism, which is a sort of partnership formed for mutual benefit. The crab benefits by being partly concealed by the hydroid and by the stinging cells of *Hydractinia* which protect it from enemies and paralyze its prey; in exchange the hydroid obtains transportation from the crab, thereby being able to

PLATE II

1. **Thuiaria argentea** Ellis and Solander
2. **Clytia minuta** Nutting
3. **Clytia edwardsii** Nutting
4. **Bougainvillia carolinensis** McCrady
5. **Obelia commissuralis** McCrady
6. **Plumularia inermis** Nutting
7. **Obelia flabellata** Hincks
8. **Gonothyrea loveni** Allman
9. **Obelia longissima** Pallas
10. **Sertularia pumila** Linne
11. **Obelia gelatinosa** Pallas
12. **Halecium gracile** Verrill
13. **Thuiaria cupressina** Linne
14. **Plumularia alternata** Nutting
15. **Campanularia verticillata** Linne
16. **Plumularia floridana** Nutting

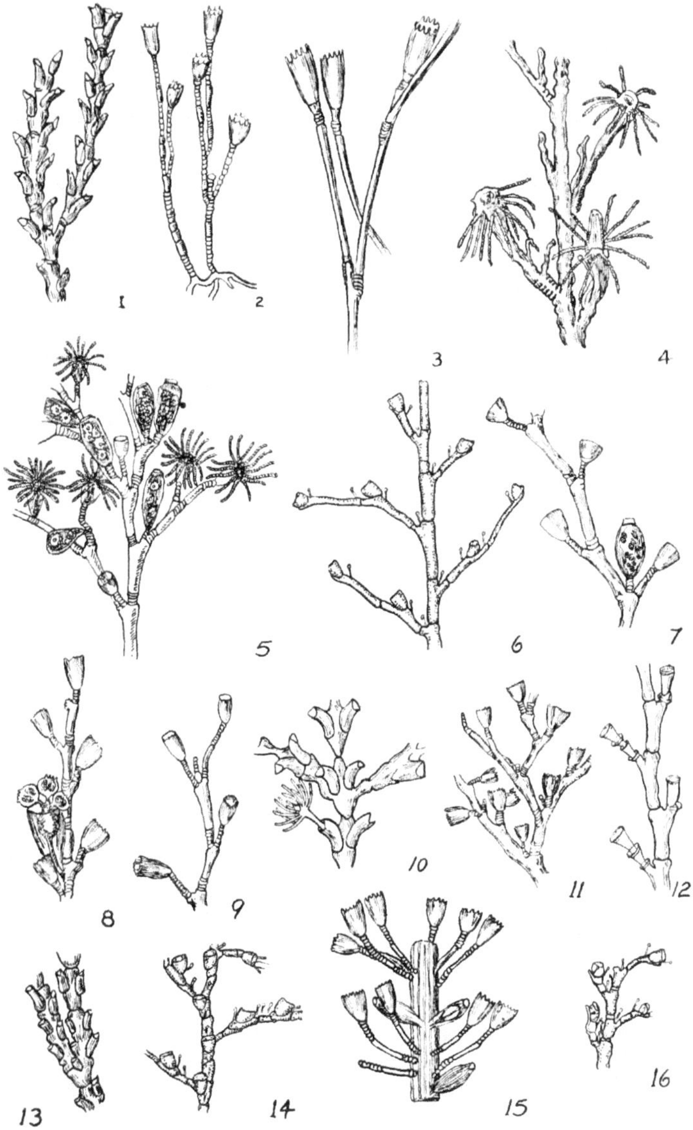
1
2
3
4
5
6
7
8
9
10
11
12
13
14
15
16

procure a better food supply (microscopic organisms) than if it were rooted to one spot.

Hydractinia is found in shallow water in tide pools, inlets, and like situations, also in deeper water off the coast at least to 26 fathoms.

Tubularia crocea Agassiz (Sea Strawberries)

PLATE III. Fig. 3

This hydroid grows in large clusters; The stems are smooth, about six inches in height and each is surmounted with a flower-like head of deep pink. This color gives the local name "Sea Strawberries." The reproductive zooids are not liberated as free medusae (jellyfish) but remain attached to the stem like a bunch of grapes.

It grows on wharves, wrecks, driftwood, etc., and occasionally on the back of Spider Crabs, from New England to the Carolinas; it is more frequent in bays and inlets than in the open ocean. After storms this hydroid is frequently cast up on the beach, either loose or attached to driftwood.

It is sometimes found in winter, but the polyp has usually contracted within the tube during that season.

Bougainvillia carolinensis McCrady

PLATE II. Fig. 4

Branched; up to 12 inches in height although usually less; nutritive polyps (hydranths) grow on both main stem and branches; annulations (rings) on stalk below the polyp. Polyp with single band of tentacles above which there is a conical shaped structure known as the proboscis bearing the mouth; the proboscis is occasionally saucer-shaped; color usually reddish brown.

Reproductive polyps (gonosomes) in clusters on main stalk and branches; mature medusae (jellyfish) break off and become free swimming.

The hydroid is frequently found attached to woodwork from Cape Cod southward.

For medusa of this species see page 54.

Eudendrium ramosum Linne

PLATE III. Fig. 9

Much branched; up to six inches in height; main stem fascicled (compound, apparently made up of a bundle of stems); annulations (rings) at base of branches only; in many respects resembles *Bougainvillia*, but distinguished from it by its more trumpet-shaped proboscis.

Two types of reproductive polyps (gonosomes); male polyps red and usually found in clusters below the nutritive polyp; female ones orange and pyriform; does not produce free medusae.

Labrador to North Carolina.

Pennaria tiarella McCrady

Fig. 2

Much branched; about six inches in height; stems dark brown or black with conspicuous annulations. The hydranths are pink; proboscis elongate;

two rows of tentacles, one at basal portion of proboscis, the other on the upper part of the proboscis.

Reproductive polyps attached to the hydranth body just above the lower band of tentacles; the

Fig. 2
Pennaria tiarella McGrady

medusae thus formed sometimes remain attached to the stalk; other times they become free swimming, although always very minute (1.5 mm. by 0.8 mm.).

This hydroid is abundant at Woods Hole, Massachusetts, and is known as far south as Florida In New Jersey it lives off shore and the dead stems are occasionally washed up on the beach.

Because of their small size the medusae have not been observed in New Jersey.

Campanularian Hydroids

Hydroids with hydranths at the end of stalks and protected by a bell-shaped cup (hydrotheca).

Clytia edwardsii Nutting
(*Campanularia edwardsii Nutting*)

PLATE II. Fig. 3

About an inch in height, branching irregularly; annulations confined to proximal portions of the stems and just below the hydrotheca. Hydrotheca large with 12 to 14 sharp teeth.

On wood work, sponges, etc., just below low tide. Originally described from Woods Hole, Massachusetts. Sometimes present at Cape May, New Jersey, in late September and October.

Clytia minuta Nutting
(*Campanularia minuta Nutting*)

PLATE II. Fig. 2

Smaller than the above (1/4 inch); branches as the above although the stem is more extensively annulated; hydrotheca small with 8 to 10 teeth.

Grows on *Obelia* and other hydroids. Described from Woods Hole, Massachusetts. Occasionally seen at Cape May, New Jersey, in September and October together with the above.

Campanularia verticillata Linne

PLATE II. Fig. 15

Branched, about five inches in height; stem and branches fascicled (composed of a bundle of tubes); hydranth provided with a cup-shaped chitinous receptacle (hydrotheca) into which the hydranth retracts; stalk of hydranth annulated and arises from the stem in a verticillate manner.

Reproductive polyps on main stem and branches, oblong flask-shaped with necks often produced into tubular extensions with terminal openings. No free swimming medusae are found in this genus.

Found attached to stones, shells, etc., in Block Island Sound, Fishers Island Sound and Delaware Bay; not common. Numerous other species of *Campanularia* have been reported along the New England and Carolina coasts and may be looked for in New Jersey waters.

Obelia commissuralis McCrady

PLATE II. Fig. 5

A delicate form, up to 8 inches high; stem not fascicled, branched in a flabellate manner with 4 or 5 annulations above the origin of each branch; hydranths on annulated stalks; hydrothecae subtriangular, not toothed.

Reproductive polyps (gonosomes) are ovoid and larger than the hydranths and are borne at the angles of the branches. Medusae are liberated from these gonosomes (see page 55).

Abundant along the New England coast growing on docks, etc. Present but not so abundant in similar situations along the New Jersey coast; occasionally found stranded on the beach; southern limit of species, South Carolina.

Obelia flabellata Hincks

PLATE II. Fig 7

Very similar to the above and difficult to distinguish from it; hydranth-bearing stalks arise from shoulders of the branches instead of directly from the branches as in *O. commissuralis*.

Rarer than the above; known from New England and northern New Jersey (Shark River); medusae not reported from New Jersey.

Obelia longissima Pallas

PLATE II. Fig. 9

Colony longer than the two preceeding species, reaching a length of 12 to 14 inches; main stem fascicled and branched; stalks annulated; hydrothecae with numerous very small teeth.

Reproductive polyps ovate with collared apertures. Medusae with 20 to 24 tentacles when liberated.

Reported from the coast of Massachusetts; occasionally washed on the New Jersey beaches in considerable quantities in the spring of the year.

Obelia gelatinosa Pallas

PLATE II. Fig 11

Very similar to the above; stalks shorter (3 to 5 annulations); hydrothecae triangular and with teeth more prominent than in *O. longissima*. Liberated medusae with 16 tentacles.

Reported from shallow water attached to oysters, woodwork, etc., from Vineyard Sound (Massachusetts) to Great Egg Harbor Bay (New Jersey); rare.

Gonothyrea loveni Allman

PLATE II. Fig. 8

Stem not fascicled, irregularly branched, less than one inch in height. Stalks with 2 to 5 annulations; hydranth toothed and tapering toward the base.

Reproductive polyps (gonosomes) attached to the angles of the branches. These do not give rise to mature medusae, but rather to modified medusae known as sporosacs which always remain attached to the colony.

Attaches to shells, stones, etc., from Maine to New Jersey (first record Pierces Point, Delaware Bay, September 19, 1928).

Halecium gracille Verrill

PLATE II. Fig. 12

Colony branched; stem fascicled; hydrothecae reduced to saucer-shaped hydrophores, frequently ornamented with a necklace of bright dots, and much too shallow to accommodate the hydranth.

The gonosomes do not produce free medusae.

On shells, floating wood, etc., from Labrador

to New Jersey (Great Egg Harbor Bay); rare in New Jersey and not reported in recent years.

Sertularian Hydroids

Hydroids with hydrotheca sessile, that is, without stalks, and arranged on both sides of the branches.

Sertularia pumila Linne

PLATE II. Fig. 10

Usually branched; stem divided into regular nodes and internodes, each bearing a pair of opposite hydrothecae which hardly touch each other in front; no stalks.

Reproductive polyps (gonosomes) ovate with a short stalk and a terminal collar containing an aperture. No free swimming medusae are liberated.

Grows in shallow water on sea weed, eel grass, etc., from Arctic Seas to New Jersey. Common near Woods Hole, Massachusetts; occasionally found on the New Jersey coast on *Fucus* (Rock Weed) or eel grass. Frequently grows flat on the seaweed with a few upright branches about an inch or so high.

Thuiaria argentea Ellis and Solander

PLATE II. Fig. 1

Dark stem with silver branches; often a foot or more in length; stem and branches divided into internodes each of which bears hydrothecae. Hydrothecae sub-alternate, not opposite as in *Sertularia*, and curve outward so that the terminals are one-third free; aperture with two opposite teeth, one much longer than the other.

Reproductive polyps (gonosomes) are urn-shaped with two lateral projections; medusae are not liberated.

Fairly common in water from 1 to 100 fathoms from Chesapeake Bay northward; probably extends farther south. Frequently large masses of dead stalks are washed on the beaches. The species appears to be particularly abundant in the Delaware and Chesapeake Bays.

Some years ago, when marine material was used extensively for trimming women's hats, this species was used more than any other.

Thuiaria cupressina Linne (Sea Cypress)

PLATE II. Fig. 13

Somewhat similar to the above, but usually longer and less branched; internodes shorter than *argentea*; hydrothecae not quite opposite and almost entirely in contact with the main stem instead of being partially free as in *argentea*.

Gonosomes similar to those of the above; borne in rows; usually reddish in color and appearing in April (New Jersey).

Found in similar situations as the above but not as common; known from New Jersey northward.

Plumularian Hydroids

Feather-like hydroids with hydrothecae on one side of the branches only. Nematophores, minute trumpet-shaped or tubular organs containing stinging cells (nematocysts), are always present.

Plumularia alternata Nutting

PLATE II. Fig. 14

About one-half inch in height; hydrothecae not stalked, arranged on one side of the branches only; branches divided into segments, every other one supporting a hydrothecae; nematophores movable.

On sea-weed, etc., from New Jersey southward; common near Beaufort, North Carolina. First record in New Jersey (Great Egg Harbor Bay, July 3, 1931).

Plumularia floridana Nutting

PLATE II. Fig. 16

Resembles the above except that the hydrothecae are more cylindrical and there are usually 2 or 3 annulations at each node.

On sea-weed, etc., Delaware Bay (first record, August 4, 1931), Chesapeake Bay, Beaufort, North Carolina, and southward.

Plumularia inermis Nutting

PLATE II. Fig. 6

Internodes long and slender, usually with hydrothecae on each; otherwise similar to the above two species in general characters.

North Carolina southward; rarely found on floating Gulf Weed (*Sargassum*) as far north as New Jersey (first record, Cape May Point, September 15, 1934).

Medusae
(Jelly-fish)

Nemopsis bachei Agassiz

PLATE III. Fig. 5

A small jelly-fish (about ½ inch in diameter); four clusters of tentacles, each cluster with an erect clavate pair which arches over the long tentacles.

The life history of this species is unknown and no hydroid stage has been found.

Common throughout the summer from Massachusetts to Florida; often abundant in New Jersey in September.

Bougainvillia carolinensis McCrady

PLATE III. Fig. 8

Very similar to the above but without the erect clavate tentacles. For hydroid stage see page 44; not as common as the above.

Syncoryne mirabilis Agassiz

PLATE III. Fig. 4

Almost hemispherical, 6 to 12 mm. in diameter; 4 long tentacles.

Arctic seas to New Jersey; not common in New Jersey.

Obelia

PLATE III. Fig. 10

The medusae of this genus are flat and discoid and very minute—1 mm. at time of liberation from gonosome and up to 5 or 6 mm. at maturity. It is almost impossible to distinguish the various species of this genus.

Blackfortia virginica Mayer

PLATE III. Fig. 6

Bell about 14 mm. wide, somewhat higher than a hemisphere with relatively straight, sloping sides and rounded apex. About 80 long, slender tentacles with short swollen basal bulbs. Usually one lithocyst (minute sense organ) between each pair of tentacles. Black pigment is conspicuous near the tentacles. No hydroid stage is known.

Originally described by Mayer from Hampton Roads, Virginia (October, November, 1904); more recently (August, 1931) found in Mullica River, New Jersey.

PLATE III

1. **Pelagia cyanella** Peron and Lesueur
2. **Stomolophus meleagris** Agassiz
3. **Tubularia crocea** Agassiz
4. **Syncoryne mirabilis** Agassiz
5. **Nemopsis bachei** Agassiz
6. **Blackfortia virginica** Mayer
7. **Vellela mutica** Bosc
8. **Bougainvillia carolinensis** McCrady
9. **Eudendrium ramosum** Linne
10. **Obelia** sp.
11. **Sagartia luciae** Verrill
12. **Beroe ovata** Chamisso and Eisenharrd

PLATE III.

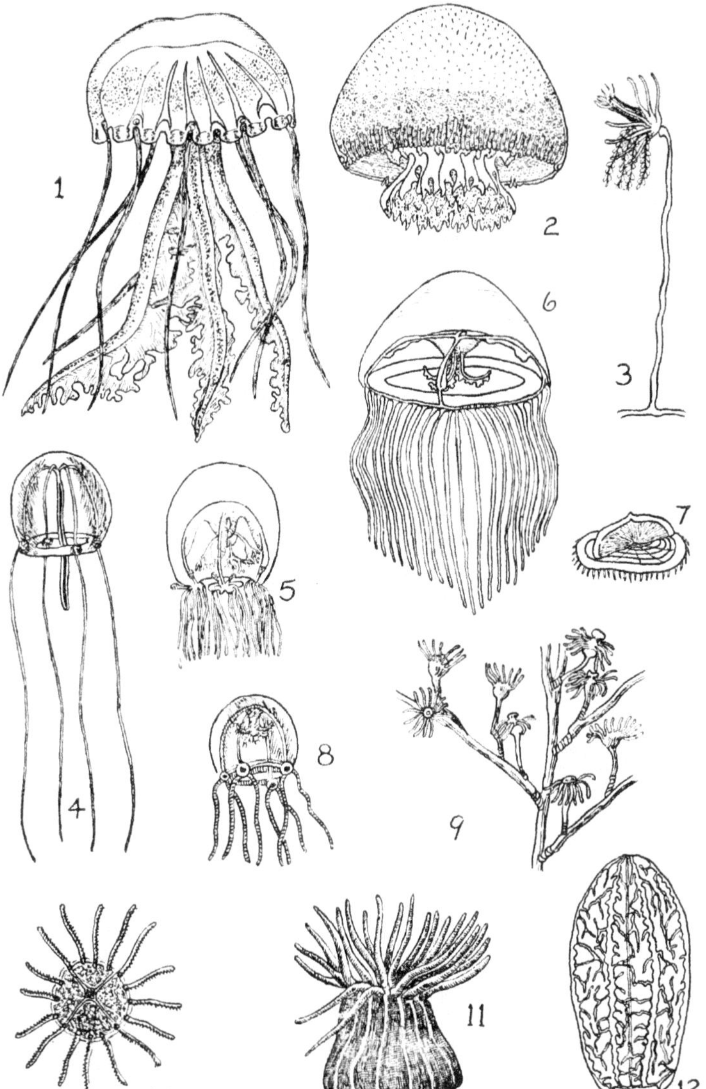

Blackfortia manhattensis Mayer

Distinguished from the above chiefly by the absence of the dark pigment granules adjacent to the lithocysts. Originally described from off Sandy Hook, New Jersey, where it was said to be common during October.

Aequorea groenlandica Peron and Lesuer
(*Zygodactyla groenlandica P. & L.*)

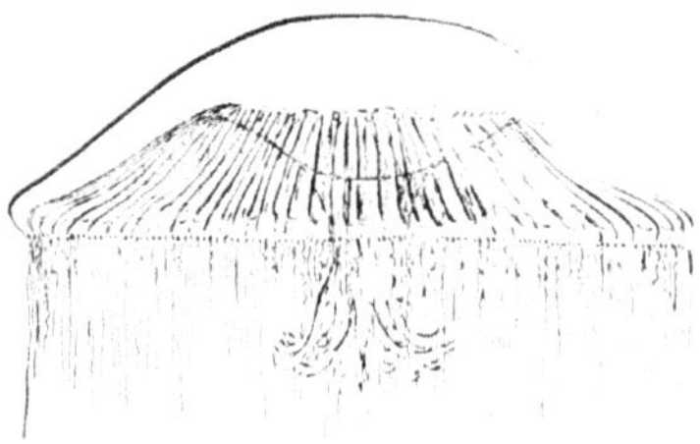

Fig. 3
Aequorea groenlandica Peron and Lesuer

This is the largest American hydromedusa and may reach a foot in diameter although its more normal size is about 6 inches. Very many radial canals.

A northern species usually found north of Cape Cod; occasionally found in New Jersey waters especially after storms.

Siphonophores

Free-floating communities made up of different types of individuals, each performing different functions in the community.

Physalia pelagica Bosc (Portuguese Man of War)

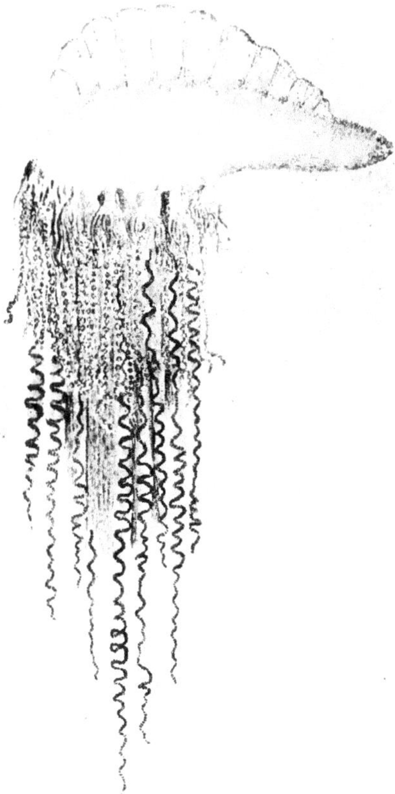

Fig. 4

Physalia pelagica Bosc

A Gulf Stream species which is occasionally carried to the New Jersey coast after storms. The Portuguese Man of War is a colonial animal and consists of a large pear-shaped bladder or float filled with a gas. On the upper side of this float there is an extension known as a sail and from the lower part hang a great many tentacles, making up the various types of polyps of the colony. Many of these tentacles are covered with thousands of nematocysts or stinging cells and the poison emitted by these cells is extremely irritating. A swimmer coming in contact with a number of large individuals of this species may become temporarily paralyzed and as a result may drown.

The float may be six inches or more in length, whereas the tentacles may extend as far as forty or fifty feet.

Several were found stranded on the beach at Cape May on September 14, 1930, after a severe storm. They were bright red and blue in color.

Vellela mutica Bosc

PLATE III. Fig. 7

Another Gulf Stream colonial hydroid that is occasionally found in New Jersey coastal waters after storms. It has a blue oblong float about five inches long and is divided into concentric communicating compartments. There is a three cornered sail. On the underside there is a mouth and a number of small tentacular appendages.

Porpita linnaeana Lesson

PLATE IV. Fig. 1

Somewhat similar to the above but with no sail. This form is made up of a circular disc from which hang short pale green streamers. These circular discs are sometimes found in great numbers washed on the beach after storms. After the storm of September, 1930, a great many living animals were found on the beach at Cape May.

SCYPHOZOA

To this group belong the larger jelly-fish or medusae. Although usually larger than the Hydrozoan medusae, they have roughly the same structure. They are umbrella-shaped and from the center of the umbrella hangs the stalk-like manubrium containing the mouth and stomach. From the manubrium radiate numerous canals. The velum or veil is usually absent; tentacles are present in most species. Like the hydromedusae, these jelly-fish are equipped with great quantities of stinging cells or nematocysts. Sometimes these animals are so abundant as to render ocean bathing very unpleasant if not actually dangerous.

The alternation of generations, characteristic of the Hydrozoa, is reduced or absent in the Scyphozoa. The hydroid stage when present is very minute. The egg develops into a planula, a sphere-like form, which swims freely for while. After the free-swimming period, the little creature attaches itself to some solid object. The planulae of some species grow into hydroids; in other species the attached planula grows in a different manner, constricting at intervals, and at maturity resembles a pile of inverted saucers (strobila stage). Each of these saucers becomes detached and is known as an ephyrula and develops into an adult medusa. A few species mature directly from the egg without any intervening stage.

While jelly-fish are able to make some progress through the water by their own power (by contracting and expanding their umbrella), they usually drift aimlessly, carried by the waves and currents, and belong to the so-called plankton of the sea. Their food consists largely of minute creatures of the sea.

A Jelly-fish is nearly 99 per cent water. This can be observed by watching one dry on the beach in the sun. After a few hours it will have almost entirely evaporated.

Cyanea capillata Fabricius (Jelly-fish, Sun Jelly)
(*C. artica Peron and Lesueur*)

Fig. 5

This is said to be the largest jelly-fish known and sometimes reaches seven feet in diameter although in New Jersey it rarely reaches more than four feet. The umbrella is thick and blubber-like. On the underside is the mouth from which hangs four curtain-like structures. The tentacles are of various colors and hang in eight distinct clusters along the margin of the umbrella.

This jelly-fish usually begins to appear in the coastal waters off New Jersey in the middle of June or early July. By the middle of July large individuals are frequently found cast up on the beach. They are often rather rare in August but by the middle of September they appear again in great numbers and are often stranded on the beach during the fall storms.

Known from Arctic seas to North Carolina; more common toward the north.

Fig. 5

Cyanea capillata Fabricius

Dactylometra quinquecirrha Desor
(Speckled Jellyfish)

Fig. 6

Frequently found with the above but easily distinguished because tentacles are on the margin of the umbrella instead of on the underside (as in *Cyanea*). Color variable, usually with 16 radiating stripes of reddish color upon the surface of the umbrella. At times the pigment in these stripes is greatly reduced, making them very inconspicuous.

This is a Gulf Stream form usually found in New

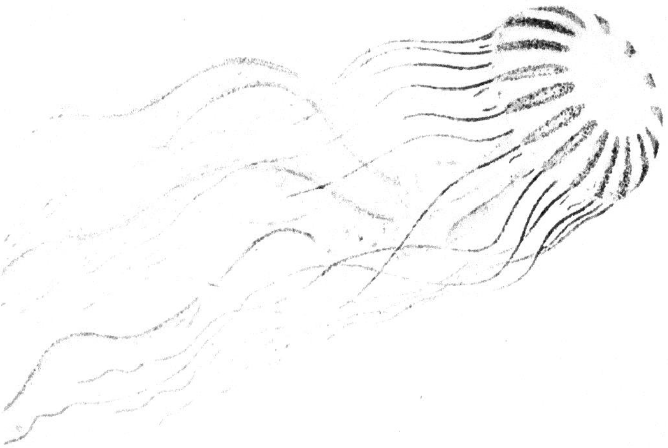

Fig. 6

Dactylometra quinquecirrha Desor

Jersey waters throughout the summer. Like *Cyanea*, it is frequently cast on the beach during the fall storms. Jelly-fish are scarce or absent in New Jersey waters in winter; however, a few small individuals were found on the beach at South Cape May, New Jersey, on January 27, 1929, after severe storms at sea. They had probably been carried from the Gulf Stream. This species ranges from Vineyard Sound to the tropics. It is highly irritant because of its stinging cells.

Chryasora stage of **Dactylometra** (Sea Nettle)

This a variety of the above species that lives in brackish waters. All *Dactylometras* pass through this form, but those living in brackish water become mature in this stage. They are smaller, the number of tentacles is only twenty-four, whereas the typical marine form has forty, and the pigment is very poorly developed.

This form is typical of Navesink River, Barnegat Bay, upper Delaware Bay and similar brackish water situations.

This variety is exceptionally abundant in parts of Chesapeake Bay—making bathing almost impossible because of the irritating nature of the stinging cells of the animal.

Pelagia cyanella Peron and Lesueur

PLATE III. Fig. 1

A Gulf Stream form occasionally seen far off the New Jersey Coast, rarely seen near shore.

Aurelia aurita Fabricius (Moon Jelly)
(*A. flavidula Peron and Lesueur*)

Fig. 7, 10

Flat, circular, 8 to 10 inches in diameter; short marginal tentacles; branching radial canals; four conspicuous crescent-shaped egg sacs in the center of the disc.

A northern jelly-fish which is an occasional visitor to the New Jersey shores. In early July, 1935, the ocean at Cape May was abnormally cold (58°) and an unusual abundance of this form was noted.

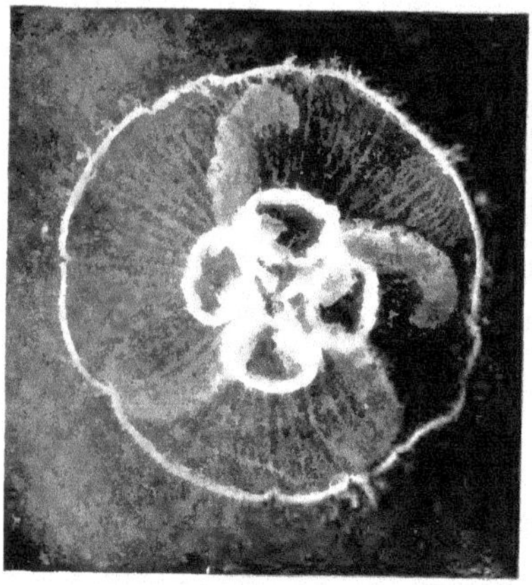

Fig. 7
Aurelia aurita Fabricius

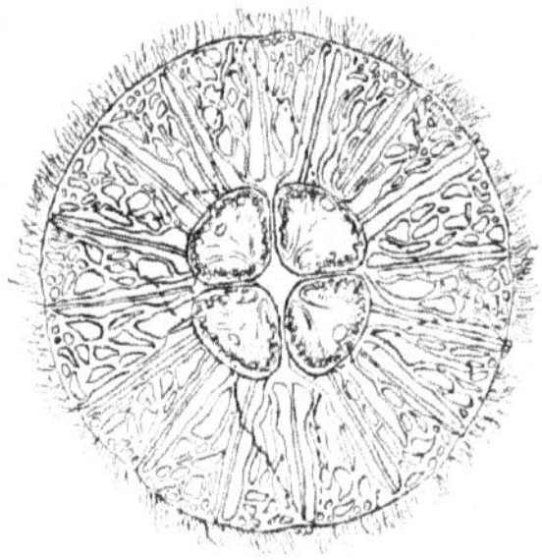

Fig. 10
Aurelia aurita Fabricius

Stomolophus meleagris Agassiz (Root-mouthed Jelly-fish)

PLATE III. Fig. 2

Hemispherical, about 8 inches in diameter; no marginal tentacles; the oral lobes extend from the underside of the umbrella and fuse to form a mouth; this hanging mouth somewhat resembles a root, hence the name, Root-mouthed Jelly-fish. Umbrella is usually spotted with brown pigment.

Common from the West Indies to the Carolinas; occasionally found as far north as New England; a few New Jersey records.

Fig. 8

Martensia ovum Fabricius

Fig. 9

Pleurobrachia brunnea Mayer

ACTINOZOA

(Sea Anemones, Corals, etc.)

These coelenterates are usually sack-shaped and may be either individual or colonial. Sea anemones are usually solitary and attach themselves to some hard object by means of a broad adhesive pedal disc. They are, however, not permanently attached and may move about as they please. They have a crown of tentacles, usually bearing nematocysts or stinging cells. Many sea anemones are very beautiful and of considerable size—truly flowers of the sea. They do not have a hard skeleton.

Corals resemble sea anemones except that the former are colonial and secrete a limey skeleton. Although the individual coral animals are usually small, the colony may reach a great size, forming immense reefs in the sea. After the individuals of one generation die, those of the next generation grow on top of the dead skeletons increasing the size of the reef. Sometimes these reefs extend above the sea and we find whole islands made up of the dead skeletons of these coral animals.

The coral polyp (often erroneously termed "insect") may be of various colors and is really like a minute sea anemone. A living mass of coral is really quite different from the dried skeleton with which we are more familiar. It feels soft and fleshy because of the many tentacles of the individual polyps.

With a few exceptions, corals live exclusively in tropical seas where the water is warm throughout the year; the most common exception, *Astrangia danae*, lives as far north as Cape Cod.

Sea Fans, Sea Pens, Sea Trees and the like are modified corals, many of which have a horny skeleton instead of a calcareous one. Although many species are tropical, a few live in temperate waters. The Sea Tree, *Leptogorgia virgulata*, is a conspicuous member of the fauna at certain places off the New Jersey coast.

Sagartia luciae Verrill (Striped Sea Anemone)

PLATE III. Fig. 11

A very individual form—olive green body with orange stripes. Grows on shells, rocks or seaweed

(Ulva) in shallow water throughout the summer and fall.

First obtained at New Haven, Connecticut, in 1892, when it was very rare; since then it has spread both north and south.

Sagartia modesta Verrill

PLATE IV. Fig. 3

Flesh-colored elongated body with a crown of sixty to a hundred tentacles. Buries in the sand or attaches to hydroids or seaweed. Reaches length of three inches. The sand flats of Barnegat and Delaware Bays are favorite habitats for this species. Known from New Jersey (first record) to Cape Cod.

Cylista leucolena Verrill (The White Armed Anemone)

(*Sagartia leucolena Verrill*)

Fig. 11

Smaller than the above and differs from it by a smaller number of tentacles (40 to 60); more translucent, enabling one to observe the mesenteries which appear as whitish longitudinal lines within the body.

Usually found attached to rocks or shells. More common in Long Island Sound and northward on account of the rocky beaches. Known from North Carolina to Cape Cod; common on oysters in Delaware Bay, etc.

Fig. 11

Cylista leucolena Verrill

Bisidium parasitica Agassiz

An elongated parasitic anemone that lives in the mouth or stomach of *Cyanea* (Jelly-fish); rare in New Jersey.

Metridium dianthus Ellis (Brown Anemone)
(*M. marginatum Lesson; M. senile Linne*)

PLATE IV. Fig. 5

Although this is the most conspicuous sea anemone of the New England coast, it is quite scarce in New Jersey waters. The "column" or body is usually brown although it may be a light shade or even pink. At the top there is a fringe of tentacles, many of which bear nematocysts or stinging cells.

The column contracts and the tentacles are withdrawn when irritated. Slender white threads (acontia) covered with nematocysts are thrown out by the column when the anemone is irritated.

In New England this anemone may attain a width across the disc of ten inches, although in New Jersey it is usually much smaller.

It has been found, particularly in the late summer and fall, attached to woodwork and shells at Schellenger's Landing, Cape May, and at Corson's Inlet and may be looked for in similar situations elsewhere in the state.

Astrangia danae Agassiz (Star Coral)

PLATE IV. Fig. 2

Coral is usually associated with warmer water to the south of New Jersey. Nevertheless, there is one species of coral that is found as far north as New Jersey—in fact, as far as New England. Fairly large masses of this coral have been dredged in the channel of Delaware Bay and in shallow water off the New Jersey coast.

The living animals or polyps, often popularly called "insects," are creamy white in color and rise above the star-shaped opening.

Small fragments are frequently found cast up on the beach. Some of these may be from some living offshore coral association; others, being very worn, are probably fossil and were washed from a submarine fossil deposit of Pleistocene age. During part of Pleistocene time (Interglacial) this coral was more abundant than it is today.

PLATE IV

1. **Porpita linnaeana** Lesson
2. **Astrangia danae** Agassiz
3. **Sagartia modesta** Verrill
4. **Mnemiopsis leidyi** Agassiz
5. **Metridium dianthus** Ellis

PLATE IV.

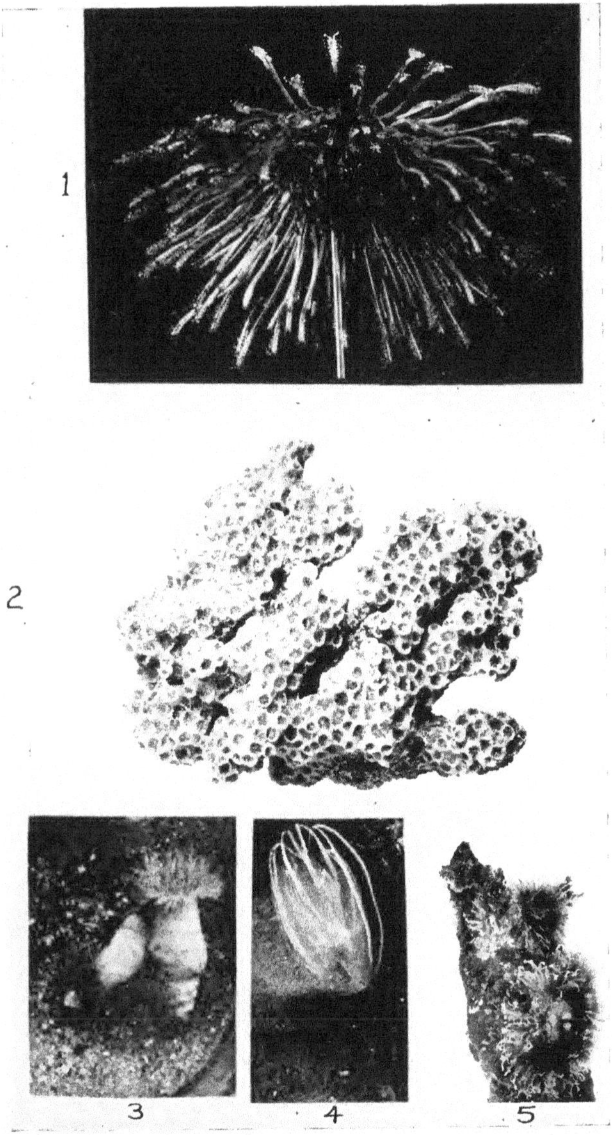

Leptogorgia virgulata Lamarck

(Sea Tree, Gorgonid)

PLATE V.

This is the only member of the order Gorgonacea found in New Jersey waters. The group is more typical of tropical waters. This species is a tree-like form with a horny skeleton which forms a branched axis, covered with a layer of polyps and having spicules of lime distributed through the mass giving some firmness to the bark-like covering.

Sea Trees vary in color from yellow to orange and red. They appear to be very abundant at "Old Grounds" some thirty miles south of Cape May and fourteen miles east of Indian River, Delaware. The floor of the ocean is rocky here, thereby affording a foothold for these "trees." "Old Grounds" is well known for its good fishing and many of the party boats from Cape May and elsewhere make a daily visit to the spot. Fishermen often bring up one of these trees on their lines and marvel at its beauty. Within the past few years there have been a number of newspaper accounts describing this new form of "plant life" discovered by a fisherman. It is, of course, an animal—or more accurately, a group of animals—related to the corals and Sea Fans.

It has also been found in Long Island Sound, Delaware Bay, off Hereford Inlet, New Jersey, in Chesapeake Bay, near Beaufort, North Carolina, and elsewhere along the southern coast.

PLATE V.

Leptogorgia virgulata Lamarck

CHAPTER SEVEN

CTENOPHORA

(Comb Jelly-fish)

Ctenophores are delicate creatures that resemble jelly-fish in general appearance but differ from them in several details. They are practically transparent and have rows of hair-like cilia which appear in bands on the surface of the animal, giving the appearance of the teeth of a comb. These cilia propel the animal through the water. No stinging cells (nematocysts) are present in this group.

These ctenophores often occur in immense numbers and devour the microscopic life of the sea, including the eggs and larvae of certain fish.

Ctenophores are more abundant on the surface of the sea at night. Many species are luminous and are one of the causes of the "phosphorescence" often seen on the sea at night.[1] When rowing through the water on August nights along the New Jersey coast one often notices a flash of light every time the oars strike the water. These flashes are produced by *Mnemiopsis leidi.*

(1) Luminous microscopic protozoa (especially *Noctiluca miliaris* Suri) also produce the so-called phosphorescence of the sea.

Mnemiopsis leidyi Agassiz (Rainbow Jelly)

PLATE IV. Fig. 4

Oval, up to 6 inches or more in length and about half that in width; lower part of the body divided into two large lobes; eight longitudinal rows of cilia constitute the "combs" by which these jelly-fish move. These ctenophores are nearly transparent but have a prismatic coloring caused by the waving cilia, hence the name "Rainbow Jelly." They are highly luminous at night.

This is the most common of the Ctenophores recorded from New Jersey. It is present in the coastal waters during a large part of the summer and fall but is especially abundant in August.

Beroe ovata Chamisso and Eisenharrd (Sea Walnut)

PLATE III. Fig. 12

Oval, 3 to 4 inches high, half as broad; pink or light brown in color. In September and October this ctenophore appears in New Jersey coastal waters in great numbers. Usually in late October during the first cold off-shore wind, *Beroe* becomes numb and sinks to the bottom. Then they are carried to the shore by the bottom current and are frequently stranded in immense numbers on the beach. In this way *Beroe* disappears from the coastal waters for the winter. Its usual home is the open ocean and it is only a casual visitor to the New Jersey inland coastal waters, appearing only after the heat of the summer is past Like *Mnemiopsis*, *Beroe* is highly luminous at night.

Pleurobrachia brunnea Mayer
(*P. pileus Fabricius*)

Nearly spherical th long feather-like tentacles. This species is . y rare in our coastal waters. It occurs in large swarms off the coast of New Jersey, but seldom approaches the shore.

On October 11, 1920, Dr. T. C. Nelson found it occuring in large swarms on the surface of the shallow water (1 fathom) at the mouth of Mullica River This is, so far, the only record from the New Jersey coastal waters. It is more common toward the north.

Martensia ovum Fabricius

Fig. 8

An Arctic species very rarely found as far south as New Jersey and only during winter months. Somewhat similar to the above, but more pyriform in shape.

Chapter Eight

ECHINODERMATA

1. ASTEROIDEA — Starfis[illegible]
2. OPHIUROIDEA — Brit[illegible] or Serpent Stars
3. ECHINOIDEA — [illegible] and Sand Dollars
4. HOLOTHUROIDEA — [illegible]rs
5. CRINOIDEA — [illegible]ds or Sea Lilies and Feather-stars

ASTEROIDEA

(Starfish)

Starfish are perhaps the most distinctive animals of the sea and their star-like shape makes them an object of curiosity to even the most casual visitor to the seashore.

While the common starfish (*Asterias*) normally has five arms, some species have more; some of the Sun Stars (*Heliaster*) of the southern Pacific coast have forty or more.

Starfish are carniverous and are especially destructive to mollusks. The common *Asterias* feeds on oysters and its unusual method of procuring its food is described on page .

The mouth of the starfish is at the center of the under side. This leads into the stomach which occupies the center of the disc with projections (caeca) into the various arms.

Extending from the mouth to the tips of the various arms are grooves known as ambulacral grooves, one on each arm. In these grooves are situated a great number of small tube-like processes

PLATE VI

1. **Asterias forbesi** Desor
2. **Leptasterias tenera compta** Stimpson
3. **Ophiopholis aculeata** Linne
4. **Amphipholis squamata** Delle Chiaje
5. " " " "
6. **Ophioderma brevispina** Say
7. **Henricia sanguinolenta** Müller
8. **Astropecten americana** Verrill
9. **Arbacia punctulata** Lamarck
10. **Strongylocentrotus drobachiensis** Müller

PLATE VI.

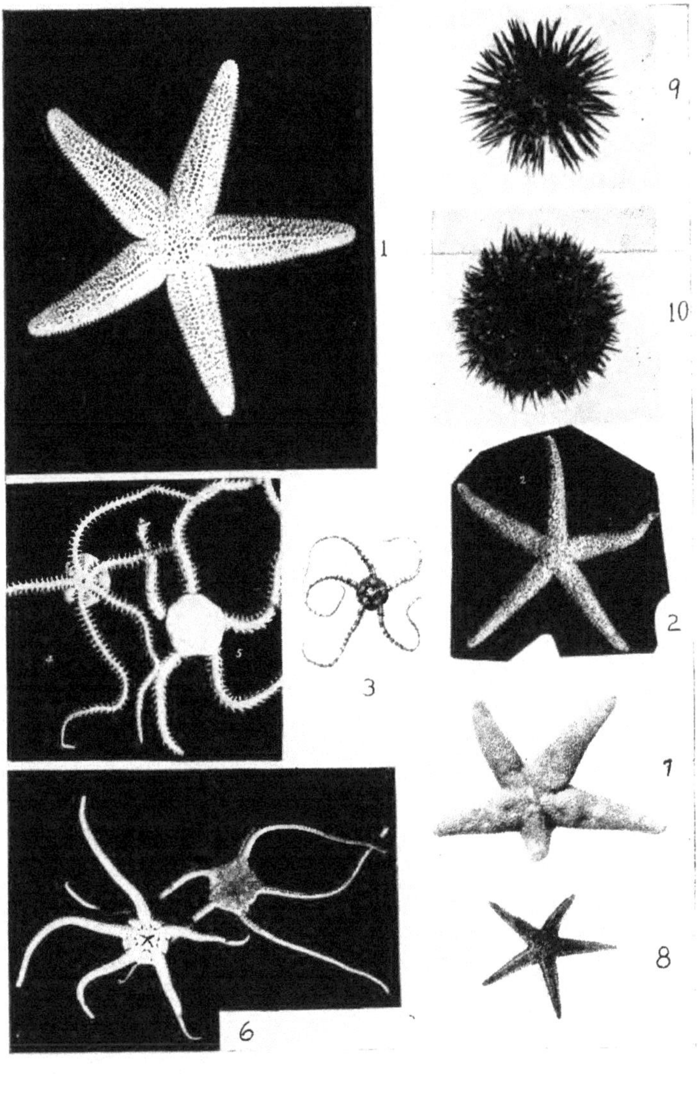

with or without terminal suckers; these are the tube feet—the locomotive organs of the starfish.

On the upper side of the animal there is a small circular sieve-like structure, frequently colored differently from the rest of the animal. This is the madreporic plate. Water enters the body of the starfish through this plate and is carried by a series of canals ultimately to the tube feet. A complicated system made up of a valve, reservoir and various muscles regulates the passage of water through these canals and thereby governs the movement of the tube feet.

Asterias forbesi Desor (Common Starfish)

PLATE VI, Fig. 1; PLATE VII; Fig. 12

This is the common starfish of the Atlantic coast from Massachusetts to Florida. Although not abundant along the sandy shores of New Jersey, it thrives on the mussel bottom of many of the fishing grounds offshore; after storms starfish are frequently found cast up on the beach.

The starfish is one of the greatest enemies of the oyster and a great menace to that industry. Every year starfish kill thousands of young oysters and consequently cause a great financial loss to oystermen all along the coast.

The starfish's method of attack is unique. It seizes the oyster (or other bivalve) with the tube feet of its opposite arms attached to opposite shells of the oyster. The starfish is then able to exert a tremendous force (more than 1300 grams) and in a short time the muscles of the oyster that keep the shell closed (adductor muscles) become fatigued and relaxed, and consequently the valves hang loosely.

The mouth of the starfish is small and it is therefore impossible for the animal to take much of its food directly through the mouth. So, the hungry starfish everts its sac-like stomach through its mouth and places it between the two shells of the oyster. Then digestive juices are secreted and the oyster is digested and absorbed. Finally, the stomach is

Fig. 12
Six-armed Starfish (**Asterias forbesii** Desor)

withdrawn from between the oyster shells and is returned within the body of the starfish. Rather a peculiar method of eating, but a highly destructive one to the victim! (Plate VII).

The oyster grounds of Long Island Sound are particularly troubled with starfish. Fortunately the great oyster beds of Maurice River Cove (Delaware Bay) are relatively free from these pests, although

PLATE VII.

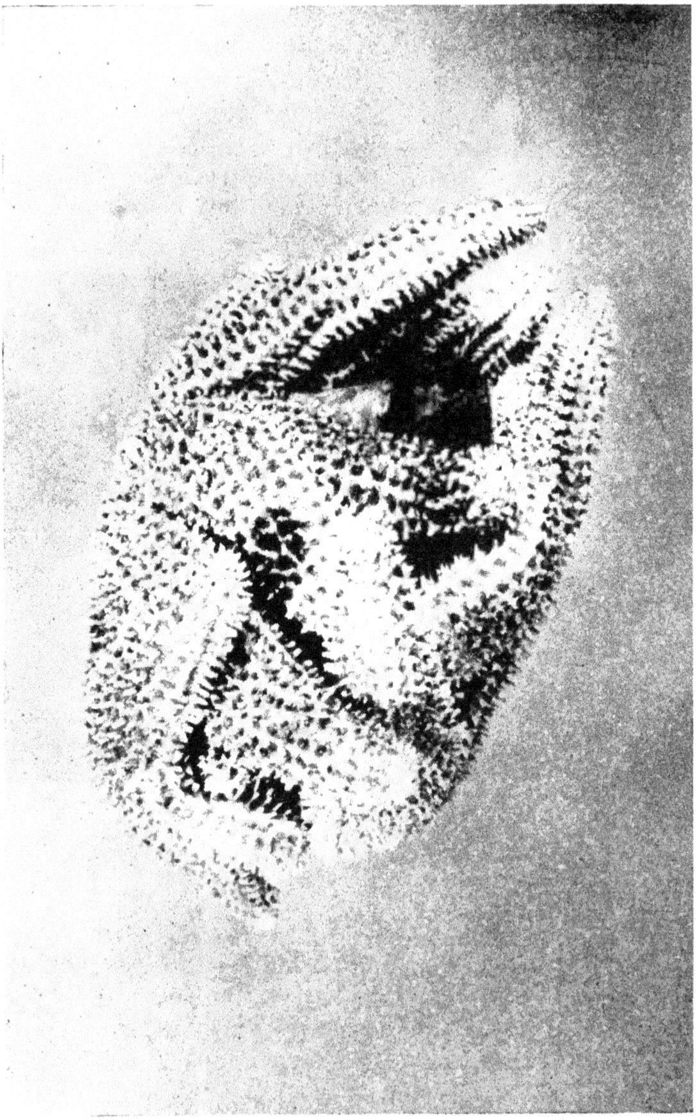

Starfish devouring an oyster

at times, probably due to an increased salinity caused by drought, they become very abundant.

The usual number of rays of this starfish is five; however variations from one to eight are occasionally found. Starfish possess the power of regeneration—that is if an arm is injured or broken off, it will usually grow back again. The new arm may be very small or rudimentary, thereby accounting for numbers less than five; or, two arms may grow in the place of a single injury, thereby causing freaks of six, seven or eight arms.

Asterias vulgaris Verrill (Northern Starfish)

Common along the northern coast from Labrador to Massachusetts. In Long Island Sound it is less common than the above species (*A. forbesi*) and is found only in deeper water. Off New Jersey it is usually larger than the above and lives in deeper water, although the two are not infrequently found in the same association.

The following key [1] will distinguish the common starfish (*A. forbesi*) from the northern starfish (*A. vulgaris*), although they are very closely related and should probably be regarded merely as varieties of a single species:

Rays blunt at the ends; skeleton quite firm; spines scattered, pedicellariae (Small scissor-like spines) near ambulacral grooves short and broad; madreporic plate usually orange. .... *A. forbesi*

1) W. R. Coe: The Echinoderms of Connecticut. Conn. Geol. and Nat. Hist. Surv. Bull. 19 p. 59 (1912).

Rays pointed at the ends; skeleton rather soft; spines scattered, but often forming a rather distinct median longitudinal row on the aboral side of each ray; pedicellariae near ambulacral groove slender; madreporic plate pale yellow. ....A. *vulgaris*

Lepasterias tenera form **compta** Stimpson (Slender Armed Starfish)

PLATE VI. Fig. 2

Rays nearly cylindrical, tapering and slender. *A. tenera* was described from Massachusetts Bay, *A. compta* from off New Jersey. These represent two forms of the same species which range from Nova Scotia to the mouth of Chesapeake Bay in fairly deep water (10 to 129 fathoms). Off New Jersey records are scarce and only from water greater than 20 fathoms.

Henricia sanguinolenta Müller (Blood Starfish)

PLATE VI. Fig. 7

Disc and rays comparatively smooth; usually brilliant red in color above and orange below. Like the above this species is of northern distribution, being fairly abundant and of large size from Labrador to Maine. Farther south it becomes smaller and is found only in cold, deep water between Cape Cod and Cape Hatteras.

It is fairly common at "Old Grounds" off Indian

River, Delaware, in about 110 feet of water where the bottom temperature is unusually low. It rarely reaches 4 inches in diameter this far south.

Astropecten americanus Verrill

PLATE VI. Fig. 8

Body flat, the arms long, narrow and sharp-pointed bordered with a row of conspicuous large plates; color yellow.

A common starfish of deep water: known to live 75 miles off Cape May; occasionally brought in by the deep sea fishing boats.

OPHIUROIDEA

(Brittle Stars or Serpent Stars)

The animals of this group differ from the true starfish (Asteroidea) in that the arms are quite distinct from the body and there are no extensions of the body organs into them. These arms are very flexible and serpent-like, hence the name Serpent Stars; also they break readily, hence the name Brittle Stars.

These animals move about fairly actively and at the approach of the slightest danger they throw off one or more of their arms. They, however, possess the power of regeneration and the missing parts are soon replaced.

Ophioderma brevispina Say (Green Brittle Star)

PLATE VI. Fig. 6

Usually greenish or brown, more or less mottled; the disc is completely covered with closely set minute granules; each arm segment has 7 or 8 very short spines on each side that lie close down on the arm. Disc usually about ½ inch in diameter; arms about 2 inches long. This brittle star lives from Buzzard's Bay to the Greater Antilles. It is very rare off New Jersey. It burrows under oyster shells and other objects lying on the mud.

Ophiopholis aculeata Linne (Daisy Brittle Star)

PLATE VI. Fig. 3

Usually red, brown or purple, sometimes yellow or green, often mottled or spotted; surface of the disc closely beset with small pointed tubercles among which are a number (usually 30 to 50) of well separated rounded plates; each upper arm plate is encircled by a row of very small plates; the five or six arm spines are broad and flattened, and project directly outward from the arm. The disc is usually about ½ inch in diameter, and the arms are from 2 to 3 inches long.

An arctic and subarctic species occurring south to Cape Cod along the shore, and in deep water south to New Jersey, where it is recorded from 38 and 89 fathoms.

Amphipholis squamata Delle Chiaje

PLATE VI. Fig. 4, 5

A very small viviparous brittle star with the disc less than 1/4 inch in diameter and the very slender arms about 2 inches long. Cosmopolitan, but rare on the New Jersey coast.

Amphioplus abditus Verrill

Occurs at Woods Hole, Mass., and Nohank, Conn., and also in Florida, but as yet has not been found on the New Jersey coast. It burrows deeply in mud.

ECHINOIDEA

(Sea Urchins, Sand Dollars, etc.)

These animals are not pointed like the starfish but rather are globular, hemispherical or discoid. They are covered with spines which in the Sea Urchins are usually long and prominent while in some of the Sand Dollar type they are very minute.

The internal anatomy of the Echinoids resembles that of the starfish, but there is a coiled digestive tube and certain modifications due to the different shape of the test or shell. Many urchins show a five pointed petaloid design on the test. Tube feet are present as in the starfish; however, some Sea Urchins (as *Arbacia*) also move by walking on their spines.

Most Sea Urchins are vegetarians, or feed on

detritus on the sea bottom. Some, like most of the starfish and holothurians, swallow mud and digest the organic matter out of it

Arbacia punctulata Lamarck
(Purple Sea Urchin; Sea Porcupine)

PLATE VI. Fig 9

This sea urchin ranges from Cape Cod to the West Indies and Gulf of Mexico and is the only urchin ever found in considerable numbers along the New Jersey coast. The test or shell is from 1 to 2 inches in diameter and is usually deep purple in color. It is thickly covered with spines from ½ to to 1 inch in length.

It lives in shallow water down to 25 fathoms or more all along the New Jersey coast and occasionally in the inlets and thorofares. After storms the beach is often strewn with tests of this species.

This sea urchin may walk fairly rapidly by means of its spines.

Strongylocentrotus drobachiensis Müller
(Green Sea Urchin)

PLATE VI. Fig. 10

This is the common sea urchin of the Maine coast. The test is usually greenish and the spines are shorter than in the above species. New Jersey specimens are very small and restricted to deep water (32 fathoms). It is an arctic and subarctic species, ranging south, in deep water, to Chesapeake Bay.

Echinarachnius parma Lamarck (Sand Dollar)

PLATE VIII. Fig. 3

Disc or shell flat and circular, about 3 inches in diameter and covered with small brownish spines; often covered with a fine alga (sea weed) giving a greenish color. On the upper side can be seen a plainly marked five pointed petal design.

This sand dollar is very common on the New England coast. It is abundant locally off the New Jersey coast, particularly near Five Fathom Bank (14 miles off Wildwood) in 60 feet of water and 7 miles off Atlantic City in 50 feet. It ranges from New Jersey to Labrador and is also found from Bering Sea to Puget Sound.

New England fishermen sometimes prepare an indelible purple ink by grinding the tests of this animal and mixing with water.

Mellita quinquesperforata Leske (Keyhole Dollar)
(*M. pentapora Gmelin; M. testudinata Klein*)

PLATE VIII. Fig. 1

Superficially similar to the above but with five narrow keyhole-like openings (lunules) in the test. Dried white tests of this species are occasionally found on beaches in southern New Jersey, but as far as is known, it has not been found alive north of Virginia. Very common on beaches from North Carolina to Florida and locally to Brazil. It is common as a fossil in the Pleistocene deposits (Cape May formation) of New Jersey, and it is possible that some of the tests found on the beach had been washed from some submarine fossil deposit.

PLATE VIII

1. **Mellita quinquesperforata** Leske
2. **Thyone briareus** Lesueur
3. **Echinarachnius parma** Lamarck
4. **Leytosynapta inhaerens** Müller
5. **Cucumaria pulcherrima** Ayers
6. **Brisaster fragilis** Düben and Koren
7. **Echinocardium cordatum** Pennant
8. " " "
9. **Brisaster fragilis** Düben and Koren

PLATE VIII.

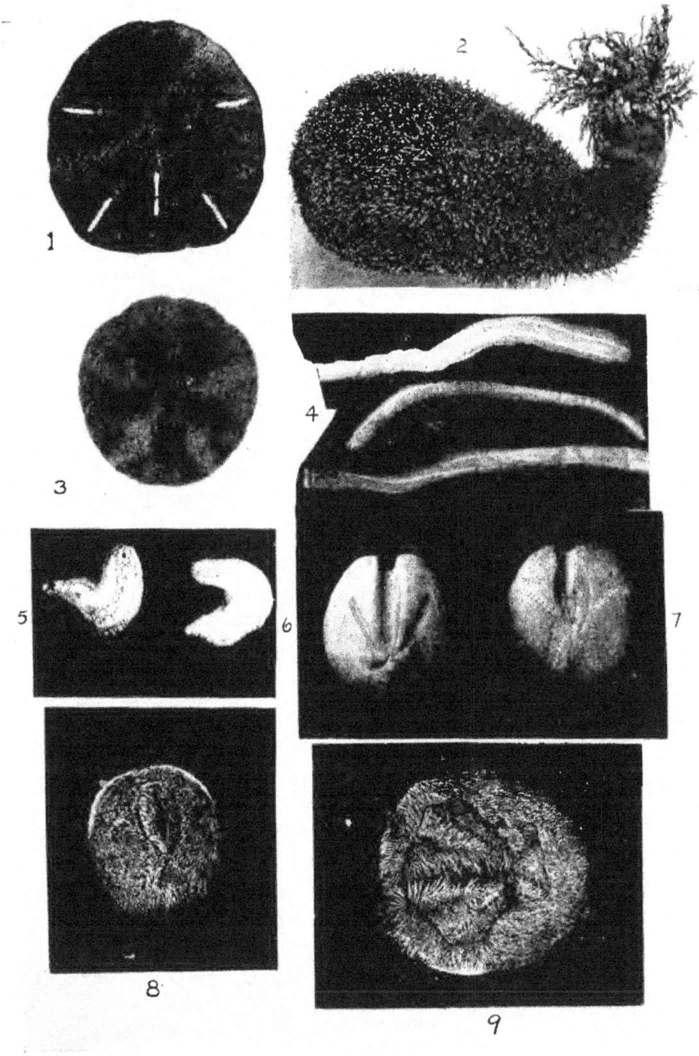

Echinocardium cordatum Pennant (Heart Urchin)

PLATE VIII. Fig. 7, 8

Heart shaped test covered with fine spines. This species burrows deep in the mud and is seldom seen alive. When they die the empty tests often fill with gas and rise through the mud to the floor of the sea; sometimes after storms they are washed upon the beach. It reaches a size of about 4 inches in diameter.

Not seen alive in New Jersey although empty tests have been found at a number of places off the coast near Cape May. Almost cosmopolitan in distribution.

Brisaster fragilis Düben & Koren (Heart Urchin)

PLATE VIII. Fig. 6, 9

Very young individuals of this species (½ inch in diameter) were dredged at McCrie Shoal, 7 miles off Cape May, in 21 feet of water (August 28, 1928). This species is known from the Gulf of St. Lawrence and the Bay of Fundy southward to Florida. It also occurs in northwestern Europe and at the Cape of Good Hope.

HOLOTHUROIDEA

(Sea Cucumbers)

Although externally totally different from starfish, the Sea Cucumbers have most of the external features of the group. They are cylindrical or elongate and many (such as *Synapta*) resemble the worms.

The mouth is surrounded by a crown of tentacles. The whole body is very flexible and although tube feet are present, the usual method of locomotion of many Sea Cucumbers is by contracting and expanding the body in a worm-like manner.

Like other Echinoderms, Sea Cucumbers have the power of regenerating injured parts. One very peculiar habit is possessed by certain of these animals. Just as the Brittle Star may throw off its arms in an attempt to elude its enemies, some of the Sea Cucumbers may eject a large part of the internal organs, growing them again when they have escaped.

In its diet the Sea Cucumber resembles some of the worms. It ingests sand and mud and utilizes as food the small organic particles contained therein.

Thyone briareus Lesueur (Sea Cucumber)

PLATE VIII. Fig. 2

Sac-like, about 3 to 6 inches long. At one end there is a crown of tentacles which may be retracted. It usually buries itself deep in mud in a U-shaped position; its color is brown or dark purple. Fairly common in mud flats and muddy bottoms off shore from Cape Cod to the Gulf of Mexico. In New Jersey it is found in Delaware Bay and other brackish water associations, as well as in the open ocean.

Leptosynapta inhaerens Müller (Synapta)
(*Synapta inhaerens Müller*)

PLATE VIII. Fig. 4

A long slender worm-like form which is very common in sand and mud along the New England coast and in Long Island Sound. It occurs sparingly as far south as North Carolina.

Cucumaria pulcherrima Ayers

PLATE VIII. Fig. 5

A small white or yellowish form usually about 1 inch long and ½ inch in diameter, occasionally slightly larger. Rarely found alive, but dead specimens have been picked up on beaches between Vineyard Sound and South Carolina, usually after severe storms. (Cape May, N. J. September 9, 1927).

CRINOIDEA

(Sea Lilies and Feather Stars)

On our Atlantic coast these live only in deep water where, however, they are locally abundant. The sea lilies have a flower-like crown at the summit of a slender stalk. In the feather stars there is no stalk, but instead circlets of jointed hook-like processes by means of which the animals attach themselves to objects on the sea bottom.

Feather stars are especially numerous on the

coral reefs of the East Indies and in water of moderate depth in the tropics generally. Most of the sea-lilies live in water of moderate depth in the tropics. As in the case of other echinoderms, many of both types live in very deep cold water.

These animals, which in the present seas are about as numerous as the starfishes, are very bony and are therefore exceptionally adapted for fossilization, so that their fossil record is unusually complete.

Hathrometra tenella Retzius

(Feather star, Crinoid)

(*Alectro dentata Say; Antedon dentata Say*)

From a small button-like central portion radiate 10 long very slender arms each with two rows of side branches so that it has the general appearance of a feather, and also a large number of much shorter curved processes. The color varies from dark green dotted with white to light grayish brown with narrow darker bands. It lives in rather deep water.

This species was originally described from Great Egg Harbor, New Jersey in 1825 but has not been found in coastal waters during recent years. It lives in rather deep water from the Newfoundland Banks to Chesapeake Bay.

CHAPTER NINE

BRYOZOA

(Moss Animals or Corallines)

These are colonial animals, many of which resemble Hydroids. They are, however, more complex in structure and belong to a higher branch of the animal kingdom.

There are two main types of Bryozoa, the upright type and the encrusting type. The former more closely resemble hydroids and sea-weeds. The common Bryozoa, *Bugula*, is frequently preserved as a hydroid or as an alga. The group is sometimes called Polyzoa.

Contrasted to the hydroids, each individual (zoœcium) of the Bryozoan colony is a complete organism and there is no "division of labor." The tentacles on the bryozoan are ciliated (covered with hairs) whereas those of the hydroid are smooth. The complete digestive system of the Bryozoa also helps distinguish it from the hydroid.

The encrusting bryozoa are sometimes called Sea Mats. Many form delicate lace-like coverings to shells, stones, etc. Other species are more massive and resemble corals—hence their popular name, Coralline.

A pocket lens or microscope is needed to distinguish the different species.

Crisia eburnea Linne

PLATE X. Fig. 16

Colonies form bushy tufts one-half to one inch high. Attaches to Eel Grass or Algae and is especially common in New Jersey during the winter months. Known from New Jersey northwards.

Bugula turrita Desor

PLATE XI. Fig. 14; PLATE X. Fig. 7

Grows in dense bush-like masses about six inches long, occasionally as long as one foot; orange-yellow in color. Small clusters are occasionally found on floating sea-weed and piling along the New Jersey shore; very abundant in water from 4 to 9 fathoms off southern New Jersey. It is often washed on the beach and mistaken for a hydroid or sea-weed (alga).

This is the most common species of *Bugula* in New Jersey waters. It may be distinguished from the other New Jersey species by its larger size and because the zooecia (individual animals) are always arranged in two rows. Common from Maine to North Carolina.

Bugula gracilis uncinata Hincks

PLATE XI. Fig. 15

A smaller colony, about an inch or two in height occasionally found growing on Eel Grass or sea-weed

PLATE IX

1. **Electra monostachys** Busk
2. **Hemiseptella denticulata** Smitt
3. **Amathia vidovici** Heller
4. **Bugula flabellata** Thompson
5. **Schizomorpha avicularis** Hincks
6. **Schizoporella unicornis** Johnston

PLATE IX.

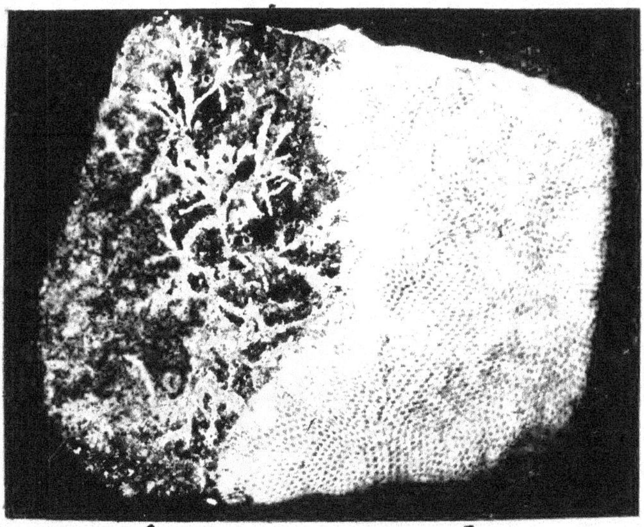

1 2

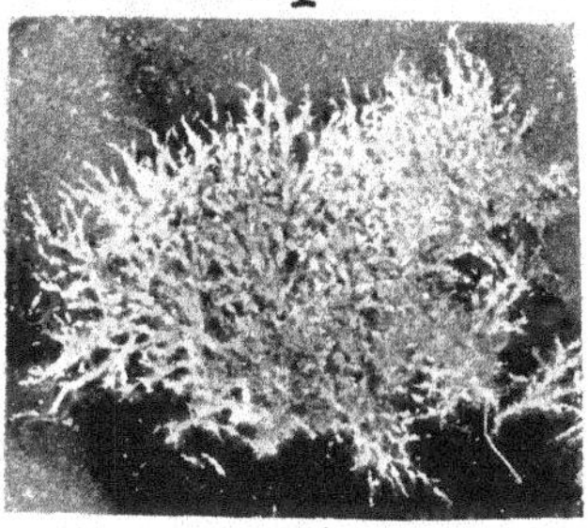

3

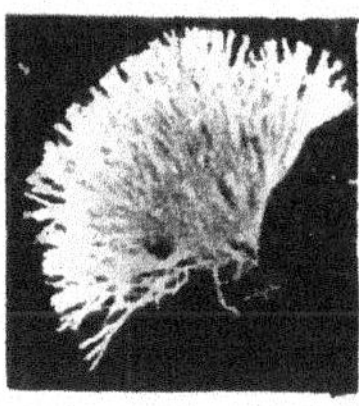

4

5

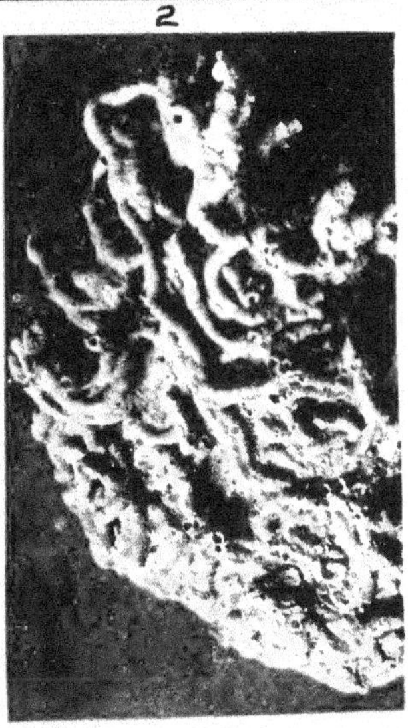

6

in the region. Zooecia arranged in two rows but distinguished from *B. turrita* by its smaller size and by having hooked processes in place of root fibers.

Not common; known from Chesapeake Bay to Massachusetts.

Bugula flabellata Thompson

PLATE XI. Fig. 17; PLATE IX. Fig. 4

A small colony rarely exceeding an inch; easily distinguished from the above two species because the zooecia are arranged in three to seven rows instead of two.

Grows in fan-like fronds on Eel Grass, etc. Known from Cape May (first New Jersey record) northward to northern New England.

Electra monostachys Busk
(*Membranipora monostachys Busk*)

PLATE IX. Fig. 1; PLATE X. Fig. 2; PLATE XI. Fig. 13

Forms small irregular calcareous encrustations on shells, stones, etc. Often radiate in growth. Zooecia oval with usually a series of small marginal spines and one more prominent basal spine. The species varies considerably in the number and arrangement of the spines and they may be entirely absent.

Shallow water to 19 fathoms from Delaware Bay northward.

Membranipora tuberculata Bosc
(*Membranipora tehuelcha D'Orbigny*)

PLATE XI. Fig. 12

Somewhat similar to the above but in this region only found growing on Gulf Weed (*Sargassum filipendulum*). Gulf Weed, as the name implies, is an inhabitant of the Gulf Stream and is only occasionally carried to the New Jersey coast, usually after September storms. Gulf Weed and its accompanying bryozoon are fairly common in the vicinity of Nantucket and Cape Cod because of the proximity of the Gulf Stream, and are very abundant on the Florida beaches.

Hemiseptella denticulata Smitt

(*Membranipora tenuis Desor*)

PLATE IX. Fig. 2; PLATE XI. Fig. 10

A lace-like encrustation, made up of very small, crowded, oval or oblong cells, which have the inner part of the front partly closed over, but with an irregular, usually three-lobed aperture toward the outer end, which is bordered by small irregular spinules. Encrusts pebbles, shells, etc.

Fairly common Vineyard Sound to Chesapeake Bay and south to the Gulf of Mexico.

Conopeum reticulatum Linne
(*Membranipora lacroixii Audouin*)

PLATE X. Fig. 1

An encrusting form somewhat similar to the above; usually with no spines whatever; occasionally with a few very slender erect spinules.

Encrusts pebbles, etc., along entire Eastern Coast.

Schizoporella unicornis Johnston

PLATE IX. Fig. 6; PLATE X. Fig. 4

The most abundant of the encrusting bryozoa in New Jersey. Encrusts pebbles, shells, etc., and sometimes reaches a considerable size and may be many layers in thickness.

Zooecia roughly hexagonal or rectangular, punctured with a variable number of small pores. Orifice or opening approximately circular with a prominent indentation; very variable in form. Usually pink when living but turns to gray when dried.

Because of its frequent massive appearance this form is often erroneously called "Coral."

Intertidal zone to 25 or more fathoms from Cape Cod to South Carolina.

Cryptosula pallasiana Moll
(*Lepralia pallasiana Moll*)

PLATE X. Fig. 6; PLATE XI. Fig. 4

Encrusts stones, etc.; not as common as *Schizoporella unicornis* and *Membranipora monostachys*.

Found in shallow water or washed upon the beach. Characterized by its keyhole shaped orifice (opening); no ovicells.

Entire coast Canada to Gulf of Mexico.

Hippodiplosia americana Verrill

(*Lepralia americana Verrill*)

PLATE XI. Fig. 11

Similar to the above but distinguished from it by its oval instead of keyhole shaped orifice and the presence of ovicells.

New Jersey to New England.

Smittia trispinosa var. nitida Verrill

PLATE X. Fig. 8; PLATE XI. Fig. 9

Encrusting stones, shells, etc. Characterized by the presence of three spines on the rounded opening. Rare; dredged in 7 fathoms off Cape May, New Jersey. Ranges from the Gulf of Mexico to Canada.

Schizomopora avicularis Hincks

(*Cellepora avicularis Hincks*)

PLATE IX. Fig. 5

Encrusts shells, pebbles, etc., at Five Fathom Bank and elsewhere along the New Jersey coast; not common.

This species has been confused with *S. americana* Osburn which may be a varietal form. According

PLATE X

1. **Conopeum reticulatum** Linne
2. **Electra monostachys** Busk
3. **Hippopoedra edax** Busk
4. **Schizoporella unicornis** Johnston
5. **Alcyonidium verrilli** Osburn
6. **Cryptosula pallasiana** Moll
7. **Bugula turrita** Desor
8. **Smittina trispinosa nitida** Verrill

PLATE X.

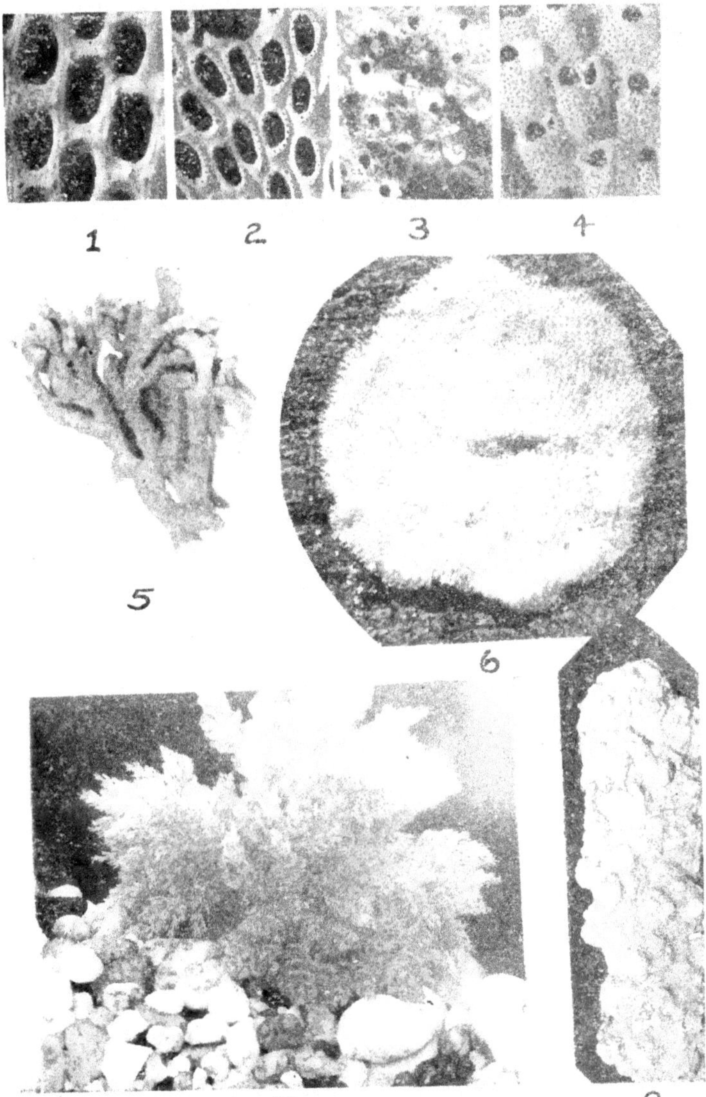

to Dr. Osburn some specimens collected near Cape May, New Jersey, are the first definite record for *S. avicularis* from the East Coast of America.

Hippoporidra edax Busk

PLATE X. Fig. 3

Forms wart-like encrustations on gastropod shells. A southern species not hitherto reported north of Florida. It has been dredged alive at Five Fathom Bank, fourteen miles off Wildwood, in fifty-four feet of water. Also occurs as a fossil in the Pleistocene at Two Mile Beach, New Jersey.

Bowerbankia gracilis Leidy

PLATE XI. Fig. 18

A delicate white creeping form with cylindrical zooids rising singly or in clusters from the creeping stolon or base. On pebbles, algae, etc., in shallow water from Chesapeake Bay northward. New Jersey specimens are usually the variety known as form *densa*.

Amathia vidovici Heller
(*Amathia dichotoma Verrill*)

PLATE IX. Fig. 3

Grows in thick clusters 1 to 2 inches high. The branches stand in different planes so as to give a miniature tree-like effect. When a branch divides there is a joint formed at the base of each of the forks by the interpolation of a very short segment of a dark brown opaque substance, which contrasts strongly with the white translucent substance of the rest of the stem. Easily recognized by its bushy character and spotted appearance; often mistaken for a hydroid.

Very abundant, washed on the New Jersey beaches during some summers; other years entirely absent. Reported from Maine to New Jersey; probably more widespread.

Alcyonidium verrilli Osburn

(*A. ramosum Verrill*)

PLATE X. Fig. 5; PLATE XI. Fig. 8

Fleshy, much branched, usually about 1/3 inch in diameter; sometimes reaches as much as 12 inches in height.

Known from shallow water from Chesapeake Bay to Cape Cod; at times abundant on the beaches of Chesapeake and Delaware Bays.

Alcyonidium polyoum Hassall

(*A. mytili Dalyell*)

PLATE XI. Fig. 7

Forms a fleshy covering to stones and shells; usually impregnated with earthy material giving the shell or stone the appearance of being coated with mud.

Known from shallow water from Delaware Bay to Nova Scotia. Frequently dredged in New Jersey waters or found washed up on the beach.

Chapter Ten

VERMES

1. UNSEGMENTED WORMS
   - a. Platyhelminthes (Flat worms)
   - b. Nemertinea (Nemertinean worms)
   - c. Nemathelminthes (Round worms or thread worms)
   - d. Chaetognatha (Glass worms)
   - e. Sipunculoidea
2. ANNELIDA OR SEGMENTED WORMS

1. Unsegmented Worms

When we think of worms we usually think of the rather common earthworm. However, the worms of the sea are sometimes very much more beautiful than the earthworm. They are of various colors and many resemble flowers and are among the most brilliant creatures of the sea.

There are two groups of worms—the segmented and the unsegmented. Although the various groups of unsegmented worms are not always closely related, they bear a superficial resemblance and for convenience will be grouped together here.

Although there are many species of unsegmented worms, they form a relatively inconspicuous part of the seashore fauna as contrasted with the segmented annelid worms. Many species are very minute and easily overlooked; the larger species are seldom common along our coast. A few of the more easily recognized are described below.

PLATYHELMINTHES
(Flatworms)

Flat, unsegmented worms, most of which are parasitic, such as the Tape Worm, Liver Fluke, etc. A few are free-living and can be found along most sea coasts.

Leptoplana variabilis Girard

PLATE XI. Fig. 3

A yellow leaf-like flatworm about an inch long by half an inch wide, occasionally found living on *Ulva* (Sea Lettuce) or other algae.

Bdelloura candida Girard

PLATE XI. Fig. 5

Elongate with anterior end tapering and posterior end with an adhesive disk. Lives on the gills of the King Crab (*Limulus polyphemus*). Thought by some to be parasitic, but probably merely a commensal form doing no harm to its host.

Syncoelidium pellucidum Wheeler

Smaller than the above (1/4 inch long) and tapering to both ends. Also found on the gills of the King Crab, but not as common as the preceding.

PLATE XI

1. **Cerebratulus lacteus** Leidy
2. **Micrura leidyi** Verrill
3. **Leptoplana variabilis** Girard
4. **Cryptosula pallasiana** Moll
5. **Bdelloura candida** Girard
6. **Malacobdella grossa** Müller
7. **Alcyonidium polyoum** Hassall
8. **Alcyonidium verrilli** Osburn
9. **Smittina trispinosa nitida** Verrill
10. **Hemiseptella denticulata** Smitt
11. **Hippodiplosia americana** Verrill
12. **Membranipora tuberculata** Bosc
13. **Electra monostachys** Busk
14. **Bugula turrita** Desor
15. **Bugula gracilis uncinata** Hincks
16. **Crisia eburnea** Linne
17. **Bugula flabellata** Thompson
18. **Bowerbankia gracilis** Leidy

PLATE XI.

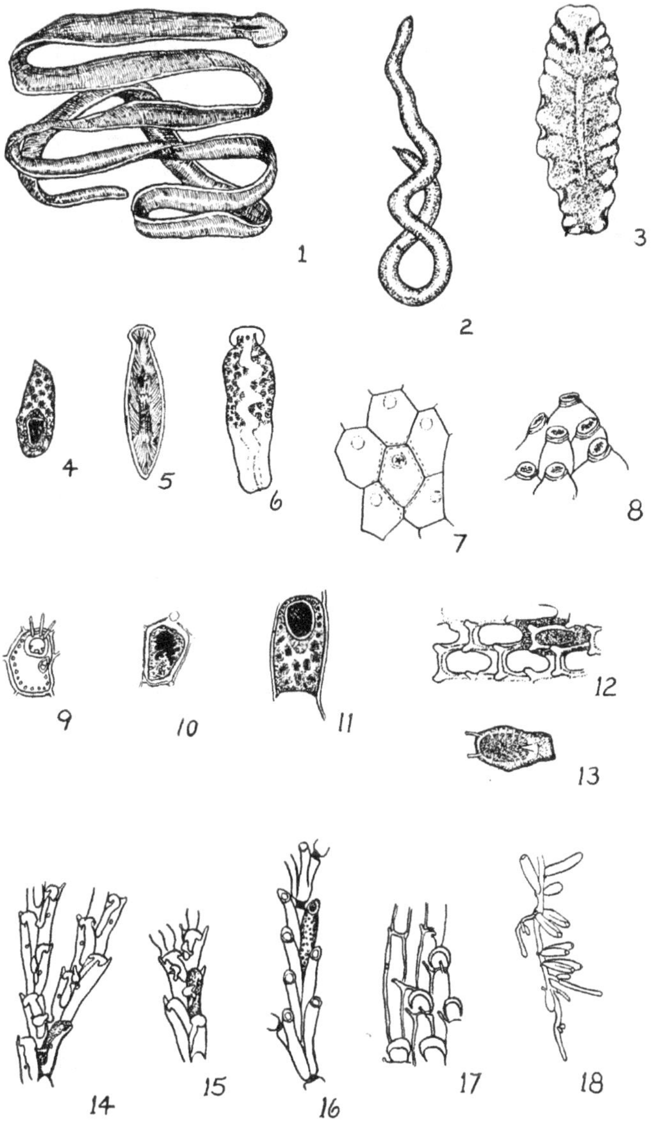

NEMERTINEA

Elongate, unsegmented worms, usually narrow and flat; characterized by the presence of a very long proboscis—sometimes as long as the body of the worm—which may be everted. These worms are carnivorous and some are cannibalistic. They possess the power of regeneration to a marked degree.

Cerebratulus lacteus Leidy
(Meckelia ingens Verrill)

PLATE XI. Fig. 1

One of the longest of all marine worms; when full grown it may attain a length of six feet and an inch in breadth; however, worms of this length are very rare along the New Jersey coast and most individuals are much smaller. It usually burrows in sand or mud near low water mark but is occasionally seen swimming in the water. Because of its great length, it is difficult to collect a perfect specimen. Maine to Florida.

Micrura leidyi Verrill

PLATE XI. Fig. 2

Red-brown or yellow, about 6 inches long; prominent flesh-colored proboscis. Burrows in mud flats near low water mark from Cape Ann (Massachusetts) to Cape May; fairly common.

Malacobdella grossa Müller

A small flatworm of leech-like form that lives as a commensal in the Clam (*Venus mercenaria*) and other bivalves.

NEMATHELMINTHES
(Round Worms, Thread Worms)

Round, unsegmented worms, a large number of which are parasitic. However, great quantities of minute thread worms are to be found in sea water. If one examines a few drops of sea water under a microscope, particularly water containing some algae or sea weeds, one can see these tiny thread worms constantly coiling and uncoiling themselves. Many species have been described, but since they are all very minute and difficult to determine, they are not discussed here.

CHAETOGNATHA
(Glass Worms)

Elongate, unsegmented worms with two or three pairs of fins.

Sagitta elegans Verrill (Arrow Worm; Glass Worm)

Slender, transparent and very minute (about 3 mm. long); three pairs of fins. Various species of *Sagitta*, often of larger size, are abundant in all seas. *S. elegans* is known from Chesapeake Bay northward.

SIPULCULOIDEA

Unsegmented worms usually made up of two divisions—a slender head portion (introvert) which can be retracted within a thicker posterior portion.

Phascolosoma gouldi Pourtales

PLATE XII. Fig. 8

About 6 inches in length; occasionally dredged off the New Jersey coast.

2. Segmented Worms

The segmented worms (Annelids) are composed of a series of ring-like segments, each segment containing a complete set of internal organs. The most conspicuous marine annelids belong to the class Polychaeta (meaning many bristles). These worms possess a pair of leg-like structures (parapodia) on each segment; on each parapodium there are numerous bristles (chaetae) usually in two bundles.

The annelid worms are much higher in the scale of animal life than the unsegmented worms. They have better sense organs, a well developed nervous system as well as a digestive system and blood vessels.

Most annelids burrow in the sand or mud; some build tubes of sand or shell. Certain species can be found swimming on the surface of the sea especially at night. Some worms are carnivorous, while others are vegetarian. Many ingest mud and obtain their nourishment from the minute organic particles included therein.

Another group of annelids, the Oligochaeta, includes the common Earthworm. These have no parapodia and only a few small bristles. Although most species are terrestrial or of fresh water, a few are marine. However, they are inconspicuous and are not included here.

Still another group, the Hirunidea, includes the Leeches. These possess a conspicuous terminal sucker at each end. While most of the species live in fresh water, many are marine and occasionally they are seen attached to a fish or free swimming.

ANNELIDA

Lepidonotus squamatus Linne

Fig. 15

Flat, about one inch long, usually brown in color, covered with twelve pairs of rough scales. Often found on underside of stones or in dead shells; common along the New Jersey coast from between the tides to ten fathoms or more. Known from Delaware to Labrador; probably extends farther south also. When disturbed it rolls itself into a ball.

Lepidonotus sublaevis Verrill

Similar to the above except that the twelve pairs of scales are smooth and lighter in color.

Harmothoe imbricata Linne

Similar to the above except with sixteen pairs of smooth scales; not as common as *Lepidonotus* but known from Delaware Bay to the Arctic. In New Jersey it is known from shallow water to 84 feet.

Fig. 13
Eupomotus dianthus
Verrill

Fig. 14
Sabellaria vulgaris
Verrill

Fig. 15
Lepidonotus squamatus
Linne

Fig. 16
Aphrodita hastata Moore

Aphrodita hastata Moore (Sea Mouse)

Fig. 16

Elliptical, about 5 inches long and 1½ inches wide. Characterized by a thick growth of setae which form a fur-like coating on its back; beautifully iridescent in color.

Lives in the mud below low tide along the New England and New Jersey shore. Occasionally washed upon the beach after storms.

Nereis pelagica Linne (Clam Worm)

PLATE XIII. Fig. 7; Fig. 17

Red-brown, up to five inches long; body widest at the middle. Head with pair of tentacles and four pairs of cirri (hair-like structures).

Very common in shallow water along the New England coast. Present along the New Jersey coast but not as abundant as *N. limbata*; reported as far south as South Carolina. Found among mussels, under stones, etc., from between the tides to deep water. Females longer than males. Used as bait as are all species of *Nereis*.

Nereis limbata Ehlers [1]

PLATE XIII. Fig. 3

Usually shorter than the above and always widest at the anterior end instead of at the middle (as *pelagica*). Common all along the New Jersey coast and especially abundant in the oyster beds of Delaware Bay.

---

[1] One phase of this species is very similar to the European *Nereis dumerilii* Audouin and Milne-Edwards and it is possible that some of the records of *N. dumerilii* from the east coast of the United States are really *N. Limbata*. The following key, kindly furnished by Dr. J. Percy Moore, will help the more technical reader to identify the three species of *Nereis* found along the New Jersey coast:

Notocirral lobe of parapodia enlarged and foliacious
  Foliacious lobes broad ovate and on all parapodia nearly to the anterior end .... *N. virens*
  Foliacious lobes more or less narrow and elongate (lingulate and confined to middle and posterior segments .... *N. limbata*
Notocirral lobe not foliacious but simply cirriform .... *N. pelagica*

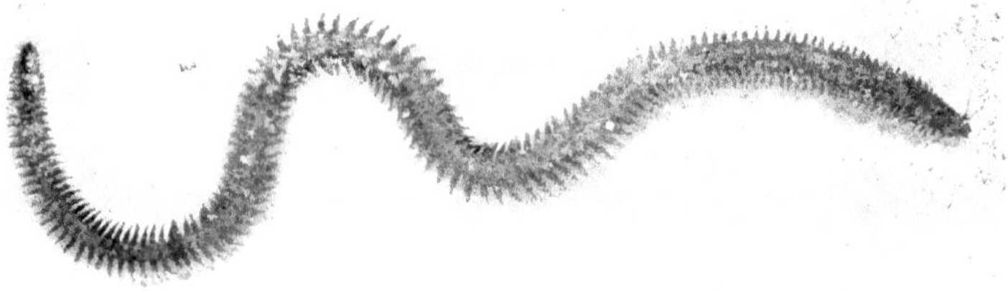

Fig. 17

Nereis pelagica Linne

Nereis virens Sais

Larger than the above two, sometimes reaching 18 inches; flesh-colored with a greenish sheen. A common New England species that is occasionally found along the New Jersey coast.

Nepthys incisa Malmgren
(*Nepthys ingens Stimpson*)

PLATE XIII. Fig. 6

Up to six inches in length and 1/4 inch in diameter. Body white with red blood vessel visible on dorsal side; appendages dark brown or black. Very active, burrowing in mud or sand between the tides and in shallow water. Delaware Bay to Bay of Fundy; fairly common in Cape May Harbor, New Jersey.

Nepthys picta Ehlers
(*N. bucera Ehlers*)

More slender than the above. From low water mark to 21 feet. Massachusetts Bay to South Carolina.

Fig. 18
Tubes of **Diopatra cuprea** Bosc in mud flats along Delaware Bay.

Diopatra cuprea Bosc (Plumed Worm)

PLATE XII. Fig. 2; Fig. 18

As much as a foot in length and ½ inch broad. Lives in a parchment-like tube, the tops of which project two or three inches above the surface of mud flats and are often covered with bits of debris, seaweed, etc. The tubes may extend three feet or more obliquely into the mud. The worm is reddish brown in color, specked with gray. Many-branched red gills are conspicuous from the fifth segment to the posterior end of the animal. The appendages are yellowish brown and green. Common in mud flats along the whole New Jersey coast and dredged to six fathoms off Cape May, New Jersey. Cape Cod to South Carolina.

PLATE XII

1. **Cirratulus grandis** Verrill
2. **Diopatra cuprea** Bosc
3. **Cistenides gouldi** Verrill
4. **Arabella ornata** Verrill
5. **Clymenella torquata** Leidy

PLATE XII.

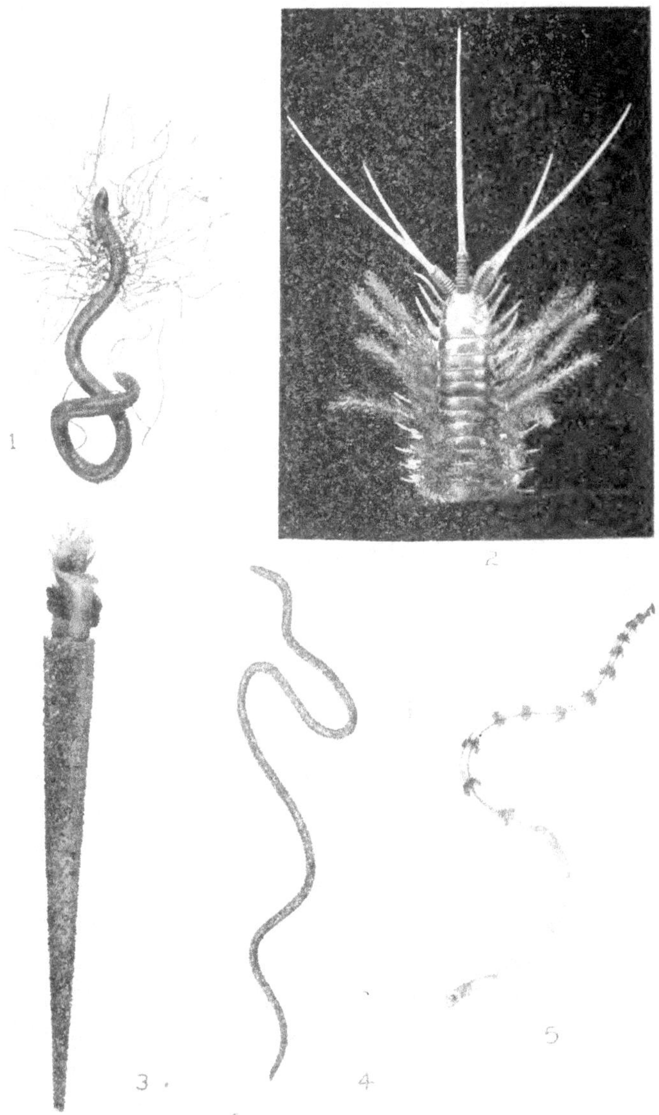

1 2 3 4 5

Arabella opalina Verrill (Opal Worm)

PLATE XII. Fig. 4

This a red-brown worm, a foot or so in length with a brilliant opal-like iridescence, hence its specific name; tapers to the ends; appendages short. It burrows into the sandy mud near low water mark, but does not build permanent tubes. When removed from its burrow, the worm coils in a spiral manner. Common in mud flats at Beach Haven, Sea Isle City, Cape May, and elsewhere on the Jersey Coast; known from the West Indies to Maine.

Fig. 19

Lumbrinereis tenuis Verrill

Lumbrinereis tenuis Verrill

Fig. 19

Very slender, about 12 inches in length; bright red with a conical head without eyes or appendages. Somewhat iridescent; resembles a slender red thread. Often abundant in sandy mud from New England to Virginia.

Glycera dibranchiata Ehlers (Blood Worm)

A long smooth worm tapering to each end; head small, pointed and with four short tentacles. Simple gills on each side of appendages; proboscis long. Sandy mud flats from North Carolina to Bay of Fundy. Common in New Jersey waters to 15 feet in depth.

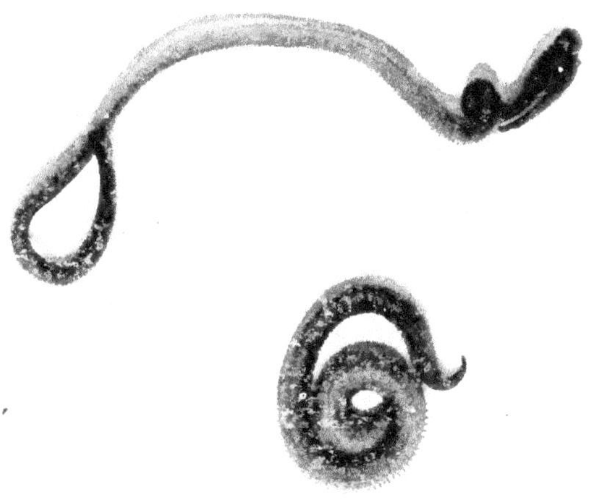

Fig. 20

Glycera americana Leidy

Glycera americana Leidy (Blood Worm)

Fig. 20

Branched gills on upper side of appendages; no gills on lower side. Not as common as the above.

PLATE XIII

1. **Amphitrite ornata** Leidy
2. **Sabellaria vulgaris** Verrill
3. **Nereis limbata** Ehlers
4. **Potamilla oculifera** Leidy
5. **Spio setosa** Verrill
6. **Nepthys incisa** Malmgren
7. **Nereis pelagica** Linne
8. **Phascolosoma gouldi** Pourtales

PLATE XIII.

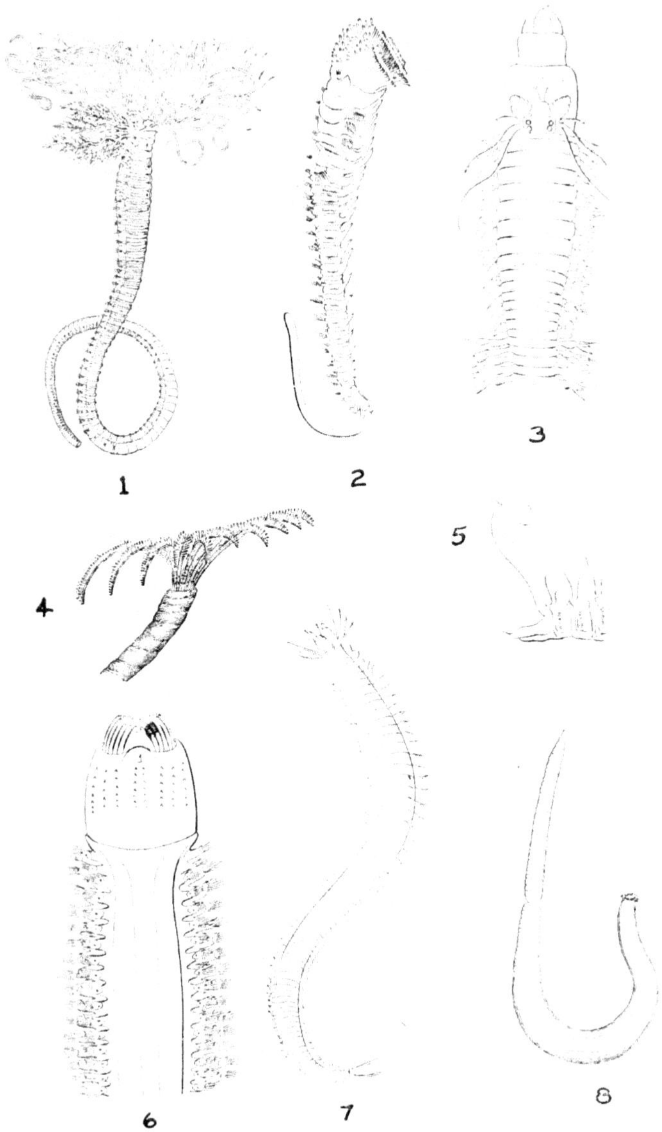

Spio setosa Verrill

An elongate worm up to three inches long; segments all alike. Inhabits small round holes or tubes in the mud near low water mark. Massachusetts to New Jersey.

Polydora ligni Webster

Somewhat similar to the above except that the fifth segment is much longer than the others.

Lives in fragile tubes which it constructs with great rapidity out of dirt. When disturbed, the worm retracts within the tube. Lives in shallow water along the New Jersey coast. Numerous other species of *Polydora* are found among tunicates and mussels on piles and in similar habitats elsewhere along the East Coast.

Amphitrite ornata Leidy

PLATE XIII. Fig. 1

One of the most beautiful worms on our coast. It constructs rather firm tubes out of the mud and sand in which it lives. The worm is flesh-colored and has three pairs of large red plume-like gills and flesh-colored tentacles at the head end. Mud flats at low water, North Carolina to Cape Cod; fairly common in New Jersey.

Amage pusila Verrill

A small worm inhabitating mud tubes below low tide line. New England and New Jersey.

Sthenelais leidyi Quatrefages
(*S. picta Verrill*)

A scale worm, up to 6 inches in length and composed of more than 100 segments. Body gray with a dark stripe along the middle of the back; head brown with one red spot and two white spots. Shallow water, New England to Carolinas.

Autolytus varians Verrill

A slender worm, about an inch in length. The intestines are marked with bright red spots which can be seen through the body wall; often found among hydroids. Known from Maine to North Carolina, but rare in New Jersey.

Cistenides gouldii Verrill (Mason Worm)
(*Pectinaria gouldii Verrill*)

PLATE XII. Fig. 3

This worm constructs conical free tubes of sand grains arranged in a single layer bound together by a waterproof cement. Body red or flesh color with groups of golden bristles (setae). Lives in sandy mud from between tides, North Carolina to Maine. The characteristic tubes are frequently found on mud flats and a little digging will generally yield the living animal. Common on New Jersey coast. Sandy Hook to Cape May and dredged offshore.

Clymenella torquata Leidy

PLATE XII. Fig. 5

Body long and slender, composed of 22 conspicuous segments, the fifth of which bears a peculiar collar-like fold; caudal extremity (tail) funnel shaped; color pale red. Constructs tubes of sand from between the tides to ten or more fathoms; the tubes are occasionally built on shells.

Found with the preceding species but usually in more sandy associations. North Carolina to Bay of Fundy; fairly common in southern New Jersey.

Cirratulus grandis Verrill

PLATE XII. Fig. 1

A slender worm about 4 to 6 inches in length and about 1/4 inch in width. Characterized by its very long red and orange cirri, almost as long as the worm itself; these cirri occur on almost every segment except the first three; burrows in sand and gravel in shallow water; known from Cape Cod to Virginia, but rare in New Jersey.

Polycirrus eximius Leidy

Fig. 21

A small red worm, usually less than one inch, with long crowded tentacles extending in every direction. Lives in sand near low water mark. New England and southward.

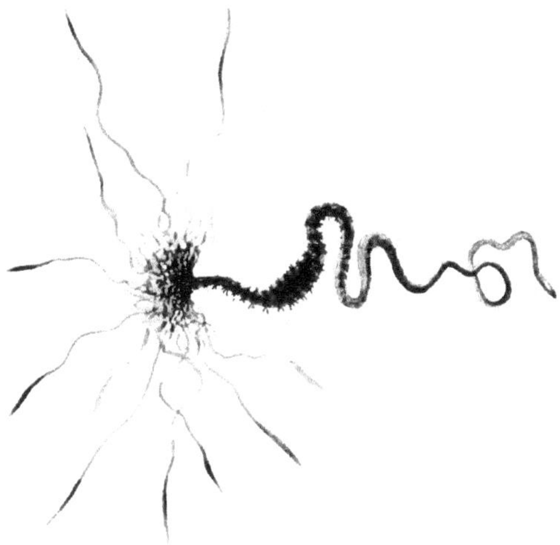

Fig. 21

Polycirrus eximius Leidy

Chaetopterus pergamentaceus Cuvier

A short stout worm with the anterior (head) region much flattened; the middle region is composed of one segment bearing large wing-like parapodia and four swollen segments; highly luminous. The worm lives in a U-shaped parchment-like tube up to two feet in length, which is buried in the sand or mud. Known from Cape Cod to North Carolina.

Potamilla oculifera Leidy

PLATE XIII. Fig. 4

"Another beautiful annelid, related somewhat to the *Serpula* (*Eupomotus*), but its tubes are tough and flexible; they are constructed out of fine sand and other foreign matters, glued firmly together with the special secretions of the animal. These tubes are often found attached to the under sides of stones, but, passing around to the sides, open upward by a free extremity; they also frequently occur in sheltered nooks in the tide-pools. The worm, when undisturbed, puts out a beautiful wreath of branchiae somewhat resembling that of the *Serpula* (*Eupomotus*), but there is no operculum. The branchiae are always beautifully colored, though the colors are quite variable. In one of the commonest styles of coloration, the branchiae are surrounded at base with reddish brown; above this with a ring of white; next by a band of reddish brown; then for the terminal half the color is yellowish gray, with indistinct blotches of brown; on the outer sides of the branchiae stem there are one to three dark red eyes. There are ten or more branchiae in each half of the wreath, and they are longer on one side than on the other."[1]

New Jersey to Bay of Fundy in shallow water.

Eupomotus dianthus Verrill

(*Serpula dianthus Verrill; Hydroides dianthus Verrill*)

Fig. 13

Forms white calcareous tubes on shells, rocks, etc. Common from depth of 1 to 15 feet. Shells cast

1. Verrill, 1874, pp. 322-3

on the beach are often covered with worm tubes of this species. Frequently present on Pleistocene shells.

Spirorbis spirorbis Linne
(Spirorbis borealis Daudin)

Lives in a minute coiled calcareous tube attached to sea-weed, shells, etc. Common from Long Island Sound northward. This and other species occur in New Jersey. Found on *Sargassum* (Gulf Weed) after storm at Cape May. (September 1934)

Sabellaria vulgaris Verrill
(S. varians Webster)

PLATE XIII. Fig. 2; Fig. 14

Forms firm sand tubes which may be attached to shells or may grow into large masses perhaps a foot thick. Especially common on oysters in Delaware Bay but dredged in the ocean off the New Jersey coast to 20 fathoms. The tubes of this worm a' commonly washed on the beach. Worm is sm: ., reddish yellow. North Carolina to Cape Cod.

CHAPTER ELEVEN

MOLLUSCA

Mollusks, Shellfish

1.	PELECYPODA	Clams, oysters, etc.
2.	GASTROPODA	Sea snails, etc.
3.	CEPHALOPODA	Squid, Octopus, etc.

PELECYPODA

The name Pelecypoda means hatched-foot and refers to the type of foot usually possessed by the mollusks of this group. The more popular name, bivalves, is often applied to the group and refers to the fact that the animals have two shells.

The muscles that the bivalve uses to open and close its shell are known as the aductor muscles and are often very strong; the scars where these muscles are attached to the shells are sometimes conspicuous even after the muscle itself has disintergrated.

The two shells of the bivalve are held together by the hinge ligament, a tough leathery substance which often is lost when the shell is cast upon the beach, and usually by one or more pairs of interlocking teeth. The arrangement of these teeth is often of paramount importance in identifying the families and genera of bivalves.

The foot, as indicated by the name Pelecypoda, is usually hatchet shaped. In some species the foot is used for slow locomotion along the ocean bottom, while in others it is used for rapid burrowing. The oyster and other species, however, possess a foot only in their young stages, while in the mussel (*Mytilus*) and related genera, the foot contains a gland which secretes silk-like fibers which constitute a byssus or "anchor". These may be used for temporary or permanent attachment. In a few species the foot is used as a rasping or boring organ and may drill a hole through other shells (as does *Urosalpinx*, *Thais*, etc.) or may even penetrate hard rock (as does *Lithodomus*, *Pholas*, etc.).

Most bivalves possess two tubes or siphons; through one the water passes into the animal and through the other it is discharged. In some species the siphons are very long and conspicuous (as *Mya*, *Pholas*), while in others they are very inconspicuous and are contained within the shells.

The group Pelecypoda contains various species of considerable economic importance. While the Hard Shell and Soft Shell Clam, the oyster and the scallop, are the only bivalves frequently eaten in our region, many other species are also edible and are used as food in other parts of the world.

While the species mentioned in this book are all inhabitants of salt or brackish water, many bivalves live in freshwater streams and lakes.

Solemya velum Say

PLATE XV. Fig. 6

These shells are very thin and fragile, about an inch long and ½ inch wide and covered by a corneous epidermis of deep chestnut color. Radiating lines are prominent. Known from Nova Scotia to

Florida but rare in New Jersey. Has been found in the mud of Cape May Harbor.

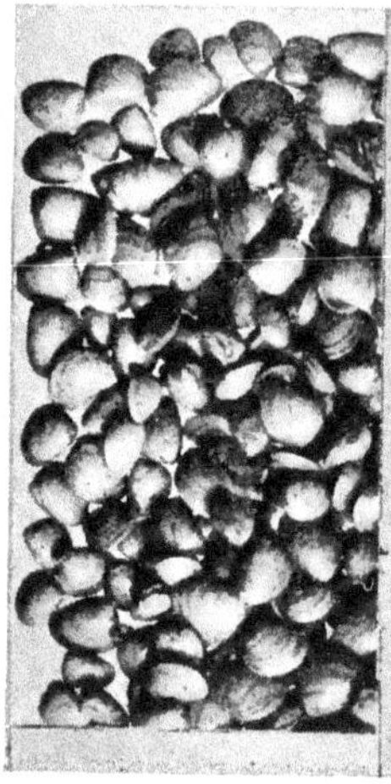

Fig. 24
Nucula proxima Say

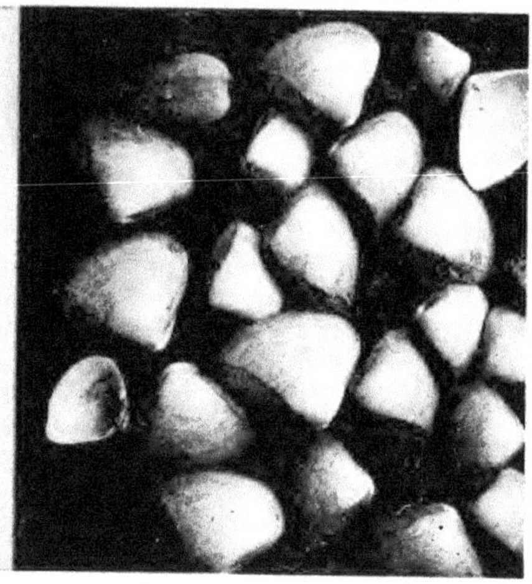

Fig. 25
Mulinia lateralis Say

Nucula proxima Say

Fig. 24

A small oblique shell, less than ½ inch in length. Its hinge is marked with two rows of comb-like teeth, one on each side of a central pit.

It is very common along the New England coast; south of Cape Cod it appears to be local but is often very abundant when found. The ocean floor off Cape Henlopen, Delaware (particularly near Hen and Chicken Shoals) is covered with this species. It is also known from Delaware Bay, Barnegat Bay, Raritan Bay and elsewhere in New Jersey waters. It is rare south of Delaware.

Several varieties of the species have been described.

Yoldia limatula Say

PLATE XV. Fig. 3

Hinge and color somewhat similar to *Nucula* but larger (up to 2 inches) and with one end tapering. Lives in shallow water in muddy associations. The shell is rarely found on the beach but has been dredged in Delaware Bay, Barnegat Bay, etc. Range: Gulf of St. Lawrence to North Carolina.

Arca campechiensis Gmelin (Ark; Bloody Clam)
(*A. pexata Say*)

PLATE XIV. Fig. 1

One of the commonest shells of the New Jersey beaches. The genus *Arca* is characterized by the long row of comb-like hinge teeth. *A. campechiensis* has an oblong shell with its beak directed forward. Radiating ribs are prominent and the shell is covered with a hairy brown epidermis, which, however, is often removed before the shell is washed upon the beach. Up to 3 inches in length. Lives in both inland waterways and in shallow water in the open ocean. Known from Massachusetts to Yucatan, Mexico; its name is taken from the Gulf of Campeche (Mexico) where it was first described.

Arca transversa Say (Ark; Transverse Ark)

PLATE XIV. Fig. 5

Similar to the above but elongate and with beak more central and not directed forward.

PLATE XIV

1. **Arca campechiensis** Gmelin
2. **Arca ponderosa** Say
3. **Macoma balthica** Linne
4. **Venericardia borealis** Conrad
5. **Arca transversa** Say
6. **Laevicardium mortoni** Conrad
7. **Mactra solidissima** Dillwyn
8. " " "
9. **Petricola pholadiformis** Lamarck
10. **Divarcella quadrisulcata** D'Orbigny
11. **Lyonsia hyalina** Conrad
12. **Siliqua costata** Say
13. **Pandora gouldiana** Dall
14. **Tellina tenera** Say
15. **Mesodesma arctatum** Conrad
16. **Donax fossor** Say

PLATE XIV.

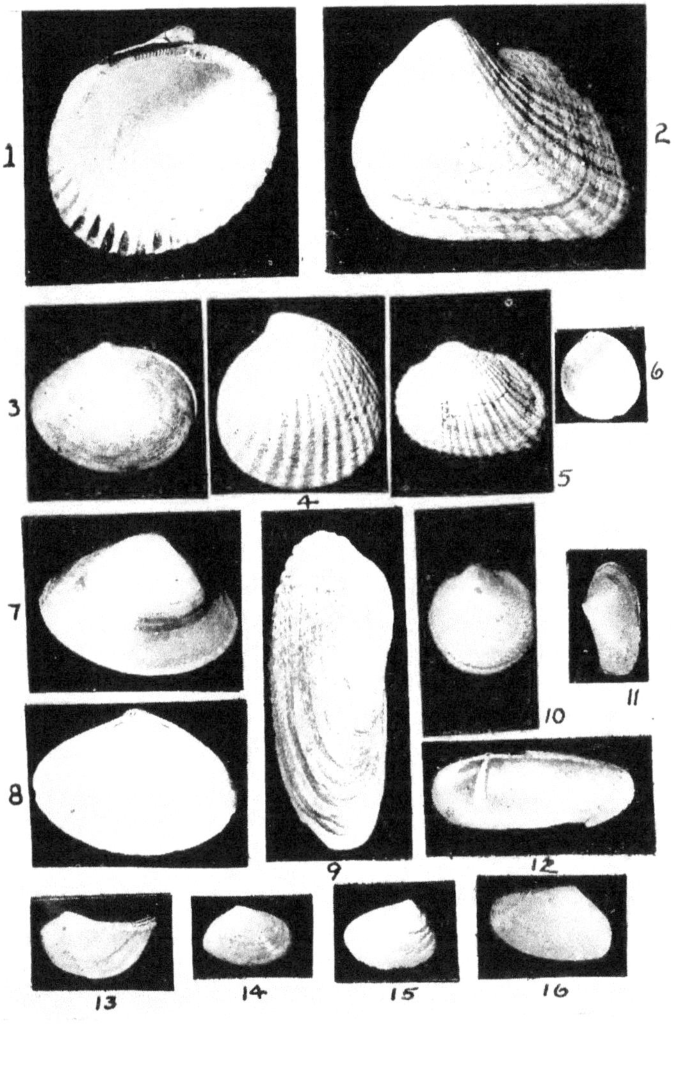

Similar habits to those of the above except that it is more often found in the open ocean than in the harbors, etc. The shell is common on the beach from Massachusetts to Texas.

Arca ponderosa Say (Large Ark)

PLATE XIV. Fig. 2

This shell is larger and thicker than the above two species. The two beaks are directed forward and do not touch each other, there being a large space between them. There is a prominent constriction on the ventral margin of the two valves. This shell is not known alive north of Cape Hatteras (except for a questionable record from Vineyard Sound, Massachusetts). Nevertheless it is frequently found on beaches as far north as Massachusetts. *A. ponderosa* is abundant in Pleistocene deposits from Florida as far north as Nantucket, Mass., and it seems plausible that the beach shells have been washed from some nearby fossil deposit. Many of these shells are worn and dark in color, suggesting considerable antiquity. They are often fairly numerous on New Jersey beaches after storms.

Ostrea virginica Gmelin (Oyster)

The oyster is too well known to figure or to describe in detail. It is undoubtedly the most important bivalve of the entire Atlantic Coast and one of the most important of all animals of the sea. The oyster industry is one of the largest of New Jersey's industries, and in a single year more than $3,000,000 worth of these bivalves have been ship-

Fig. 22

Oyster Reef, Pierces Point, N. J. (Delaware Bay)

ped from the oyster grounds of Maurice River Cove alone.

Oysters live in great beds in bays and esturaries where the sea water is diluted with considerable fresh water from the rivers. In most places oysters live in shallow water and from New Jersey southward they may often be seen exposed between the tides. Figure shows an oyster bed or reef in Delaware Bay as it appears at low tide.

The life history of the oyster is very interesting, and one that has received considerable study from biologists. In the spring or early summer, or as soon as the water has reached a temperature of 68° or 70° F., the oyster begins to spawn. The time of spawning varies considerably with the locality. In Long Island Sound, most oysters spawn in late July; in New Jersey spawning occurs in May or

June and along the southern Atlantic or Gulf Coast, it may occur as early as March.

The embryo produced by the spawning is a minute (0.25 mm.) spherical body. It is able to move over the surface of the water by means of its small hair line cilia or swimming organs. This free swimming stage may last two or three weeks. However it soon wearies of a free swimming existence and falls down through the water and "sets" or attaches itself to the substratum. If the young oyster happens to fall on something hard, it will immediately attach itself, and lose forever its cilia. On the other hand, if it falls on something soft, such as mud, it will be unable to set, and will consequently soon die. It is therefore to the great

Fig. 23

Oyster shells, Bivalve, N. J.

interest of the oystermen, that the young oyster find something hard when it begins to set. It is in many places the practice to save all the empty shells and throw them back into the water. See figure 23.

After setting, the oyster grows and in about two years (in New Jersey) will reach a marketable size. Very often the oystermen will dredge the young oyster (spat) and replant them in order to thin out the beds to avoid overcrowding. Sometimes oysters are transported a considerable distance before replanting.

In the United States, the oyster occurs from Massachusetts to Southern Texas. As demonstrated by the presence of large Indian shell heaps, the oyster undoubtedly lived as far north as Maine within the past few hundred years. There are various species of oysters (*Ostrea*) in tropical waters, and *O. virginica* has been reported at least as far south as Honduras.

In New Jersey, the most important oyster grounds are found in Maurice River [illegible] a part of Delaware Bay. The towns of Biva[illegible] Port Norris are the center of the oyster indus[illegible] this State.

The trade names of oysters such as "Lynnhavens", "Blue Points" "Maurice River Salts", etc. are local variations in size, shape, etc. probably due to ecological conditions of the environment.

Pecten gibbus irradians Lamarck (Bay Scallop)

PLATE XV. Fig. 9

This fan-shaped shell is found on all beaches from New England to Florida. In this species the "ears" of the shell near the beak are about equal in size.

PLATE XV

1. **Ensis directus** Conrad
2. **Tagelus gibbus** Spengler
3. **Yoldia limatula** Say
4. **Anomia simplex** D'Orbigny
5. **Pholas truncata** Say
6. **Solemya velum** Say
7. **Astarte castanea** Say
8. **Pitar morrhuana** Gould
9. **Pecten gibbus irradians** Lamarck

PLATE XV.

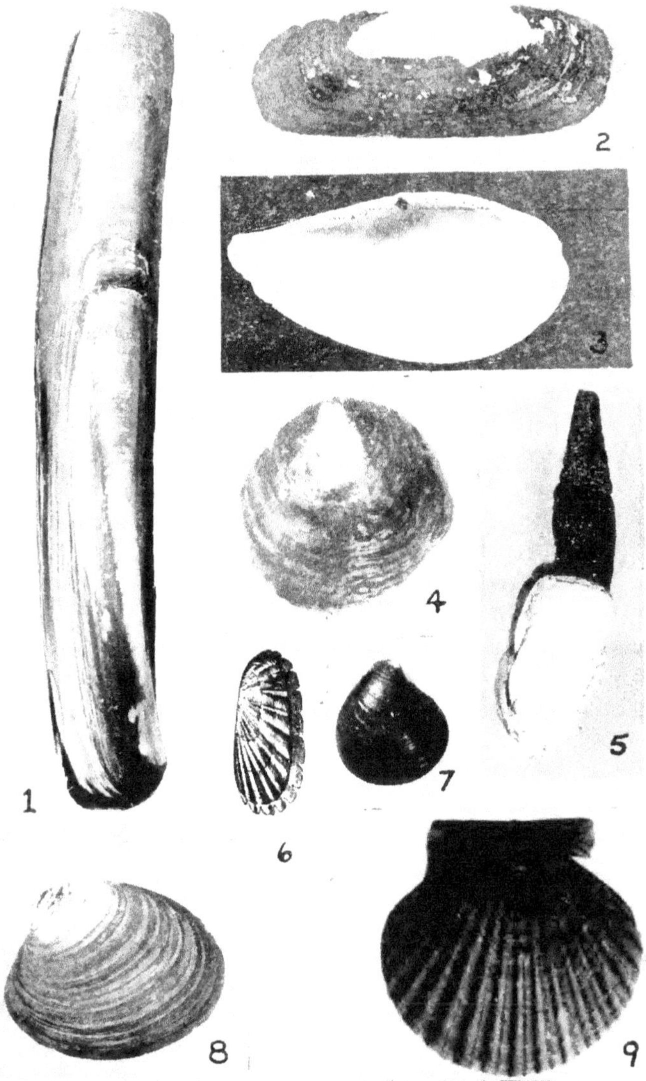

This scallop was formerly of considerable economic importance in New Jersey; however, the number of scallops has steadily decreased, and now although the shells are frequently found on the beach, they do not occur in commercial numbers at many places within the state.

It is only the muscle that connects the two shells of the scallop that is eaten and this is usually considered very delicious.

The scallop is one of the few bivalves that is able to swim through the water. By means of quickly opening and closing its shell it is able to make fairly good progress.

It is also one of the few bivalves equipped with good eyes (ocelli). These small black dots can be seen lining the margin of the shell.

The scallop lives in shallow water and is often very common on mud flats. Various varieties have been described from different parts of the East Coast, differentiated by the number of ribs, convexity of the shell and other minor variations. The color of *irradians* varies from white to brown. The black scallop shells occasionally found on certain beaches are probably fossils redeposited from some nearby Pleistocene formation.

Pecten grandis Sollander

(Sea Scallop; Giant Scallop)

(*P. magellanica Gmelin; P. tenuicostata Mighells*)

PLATE XVII. Fig. 3

Much larger than the Bay Scallop and with much finer ridges; reaches a length of almost 6 inches; upper valve brown, lower one white; this scallop is fairly common north of Cape Cod, especially on Georges Bank, where it is dredged by the commercial fishing boats. South of Cape Cod it is restricted to the deeper cold water and while it is known as far south as Hatteras, it is very rare south of Cape May. Beds of the Sea Scallop off the coast of New Jersey are occasionally visited by some of the fishing boats.

Anomia simplex D'Orbigny (Toe Nail; Jingle)
(*A. ephippium Linne*)

PLATE XV. Fig. 4

Roughly round in shape, up to 3 inches in diameter; shells are very variable in color from pale yellow to dark brown and black; especially characterized by its pearl-like nacre. One valve is flat and there is a large oblong hole near the beak; through this hole projects a calcareous byssus by means of which the animal anchors itself to some hard object such as another shell or pebble; the other valve is curved.

Sometimes hundreds of these shells showing all variations in shape and color can be found on the New Jersey beaches; the toe nail can be seen alive attached to larger shells, stones, etc. in shallow water. The Toe Nail is known from New England to Florida.

Mytilus edulis Linne (Mussel)

PLATE XVI.

The mussel is abundant along the east coast from the Arctic regions to North Carolina, although it is more common from New Jersey northward. The shell is easily recognized by its usual jet black color and by its beak at the tip of the shell There is a form with green and yellow rays, sometimes called variety *pellucidus*, and a brown form known as *notatus* but these are probably merely genetic types and occur with the typical *edulis*.

The mussel is frequently found attached by its thread-like byssus to piles and rocks along the New Jersey coast; it also lives below low water and is known from 25 or more fathoms. The mussels from deeper water often grow much larger than those of the intertidal zone. The bottom of the ocean and Delaware Bay in many places is covered with mussels, and after severe storms these shells are washed up on the beach in great numbers. Starfish are often abundant on these mussel grounds.

Although usually anchored to one spot by its byssus, the mussel may "break anchor" and move about by means of its foot and attach itself by secreting new byssal threads.

The mussel is prized as food in Europe but does not seem to have found much favor in the United States.

Mytilus recurvus Rafinesque (Southern Mussel)
(*M. hamatus Say; M. clava Meuschen*)

PLATE XIX. Fig. 12

Differs from the above by being twisted near the beak and by being striated; usually dark brown in color and smaller than the above. Abundant from Chesapeake Bay southward; local in New Jersey and southern New England; probably introduced into Barnegat Bay with seed oysters from the Chesapeake.

PLATE XVI.

Mytilus edulis Linne

Modiolus modiolus Linne (Bearded Mussel)

PLATE XIX. Fig. 11

In this genus the beak is not at the tip of the shell but a little to one side. The shell is large (up to 5 inches) and is covered with a dark brown epidermis and a tough growth of hair. Common from New England to the Arctic; known from deep water off Long Island, New Jersey and North Carolina; a few shells have been found on the beach at Point Pleasant, N. J., Wildwood, N. J., and Cape May, N. J.

Modiolus demissus Dillwyn (Horse Mussel)
(*M. plicatula Lamarck*)

PLATE XIX. Fig. 10

Beak similar to the above but the shell has numerous radiating ribs; the epidermis is very thin and of pale brown color; length up to 4 inches. Very common in New Jersey on tidal mud flats and estuaries, extending into brackish and almost fresh water; found between the tides and above high water mark. Known from the Gulf of St. Lawrence to Florida; not edible, frequently poisonous.

Pandora gouldiana Dall (Pandora)
(*P. trilineata Gould; P. trilineata Say* (?))

PLATE XIV. Fig. 13

An extremely flat white shell about 1 inch long. The shell is shiny, rounded anteriorly and extended posteriorly into an upturned tip which gapes to accomodate two little siphons.

P. gouldiana is found in shallow water on sandy bottom from Prince Edward Island to North Carolina. The southern form *P. trilineata* Say, known from North Carolina to the Gulf of Mexico, differs so slightly from the northern form that it seems probable that they should be regarded as the same species.

Pandora, while not common in New Jersey, is fairly numerous in a few places, particularly in parts of Delaware Bay.

Lyonsia hyalina Conrad

PLATE XIV. Fig. 11

Shell pearly and transparent, a little less than ½ inch long with the left valve slightly larger than the right. Anterior end rounded, posterior end elongate. Lives in shallow muddy water from the Gulf of St. Lawrence to Texas. In New Jersey it is known from Barnegat and Delaware Bays; not common.

Cyprina islandica Linne
(*Arctica islandica Linne*)

PLATE XIX. Fig. 4

A large clam up to 4 inches in length easily recognized by its thick wrinkled black epidermis; usually lives in deep water (6-90 fathoms) and is occasional but not common on the New England beaches after storms. Known from New Jersey by only one record, 20 miles southeast of Atlantic City.

Astarte castanea Say

PLATE XV. Fig. 7

Shell thick, smooth, about 1 inch in length and covered with a light brown epidermis. Found between Nova Scotia and Cape Hatteras but very rare south of Delaware; fairly common on sandy grounds off northern New Jersey and frequently found on the beaches of Asbury Park, Seaside Park, Beach Haven and vicinity. Less common in Southern New Jersey but is known to occur off Atlantic City and near Five Fathom Bank (14 miles off Wildwood).

Astarte is a northern genus and there are a number of species found along the coast of Northern New England, Nova Scotia and Newfoundland.

Venericardia borealis Conrad
(*Cardita borealis Conrad*)

PLATE XIV. Fig. 4

A heart-shaped shell with conspicuous radiating ribs; two prominent hinge teeth; rusty brown epidermis. Fairly common Labrador to Cape Cod; rare and in deep water south of that cape; a few shells have been found on the New Jersey beaches at Cape May and elsewhere; about an inch in length.

Venericardia tridentata Say

PLATE XIX. Fig. 9

A small ($\frac{1}{2}$ inch) somewhat triangular clam with prominent ribs; decidedly a southern species not hitherto reported north of North Carolina. It occurs in considerable numbers near the mouth of Delaware Bay and elsewhere in southern New Jersey.

Divarcella quadrisulcata D'Orbigny
(Dollar a Dozen)
(*Lucina dentata Wood*)

PLATE XIV. Fig. 10

Shell up to about 1 inch in length, with well marked concentric lines crossed by a series of wavy lines. This shell is frequently found on beaches along the whole length of New Jersey from Sandy Hook to Cape May, but has never been seen alive in New Jersey waters. It is said to live in from 10 to 30 fathoms between Massachusetts and Brazil; it is much more common, and the shells are much fresher in appearance south of New Jersey; it is probable that many of the New Jersey shells are fossils.

Laevicardium mortoni Conrad
(Heart Shell; Smooth Cockle)
(*Cardium mortoni Conrad*)

PLATE XIV. Fig. 6

A smooth white, somewhat heart-shaped shell, seldom more than an inch in length and about the same in height; hinge typical of the genus with two teeth in the center and one lateral tooth on each side and some little distance from the center (beak).

A rather rare shell which occasionally can be found burrowing in the sand or mud in shallow water; it is found between Nova Scotia and the Gulf of Mexico, but is more common toward the south.

Cardium is a more or less southern genus, a goodly number of species being known from Florida. The large, ribbed, *C. robustum*, which may reach as much as 5 inches in height, is common from Virginia.

Venus mercenaria Linne
(Hard Shell Clam; Little Neck; Quohog)

PLATE XIX. Fig. 5

This is the common clam of the New Jersey coast and the one most frequently used as food. It lives in the sandy mud flats. It burrows into the mud, and, especially when young, can dig or crawl fairly rapidly by means of its foot. It obtains its food through the small siphon or neck which is projected upward. This small siphon has given the popular name Little Neck as contrasted with the Soft Shell Clam or Nanny Nose (*Mya arenaria*) which has a long projecting siphon.

The Hard Shell Clam was frequently used as food by the Indians who gave it the name Quohog. Large piles of the shells of this species will often indicate the site of a former Indian village. The purple portion of the inside of the shell was frequently used as wampum or money.

The species ranges from the Gulf of St. Lawrence to the Gulf of Mexico. The large shells, particularly those from the southern coast, are frequently difficult to distinguish from *Venus campechiensis*; it is highly possible that *mercenaria* and *campechiensis* should be regarded as ecological or genetic varieties of a single species.

The shells of *Venus mercenaria* as well as *V. campechiensis* from the Pleistocene are often considerably thicker than those living today.

Venus mercenaria notata Say

A variety of the common clam (*V. mercenaria*) with zig-zag color markings on the shell; said to live on the sandbars off shore; shells are occasionally found on the beach, but the variety is by no means common.

Venus campechiensis Gmelin
(*V. mortoni* *Conrad*)

Very similar to *V. mercenaria* but distinguished from it by having its concentric ridges extending across the entire shell, whereas in *mercenaria* they are obscured except near the beak. *Campechiensis* never has the interior purple characteristic of *mercenaria*.

V. campechiensis is a southern form and in the Carolinas, Georgia and Florida may attain a considerable size (as much as 8 inches in diameter).

New Jersey specimens are very small—rarely more than 2 inches in length—and can usually be distinguished from *mercenaria* by their conspicuous concentric ridges.

Gemma gemma Totten (Gem Shell)

A minute clam (usually less than 1/4 inch) with typical venerid hinge, frequently found in great numbers in tide pools along the entire New Jersey coast. This species, made up of three varieties, is known from Labrador to the Gulf of Mexico.

Pitar morrhuana Gould
(*Cytherea convexa Say; Callocardia morrhuana Gould*)

PLATE XV. Fig. 8

Closely resembles *Venus mercenaria*, but rarely grows larger than 2 inches; shell smoother and with no purple marks on the interior; hinge has both lateral and cardinal teeth.

Lives in shallow water from Nova Scotia to Florida; not uncommon on New Jersey beaches but more abundant farther south.

Petricola pholadiformis Lamarck (Angel Wings)

PLATE XIV. Fig. 9

Shell thin, white, with numerous ribs; about 2 inches in length; when spread open resembles a pair of wings, hence the name. It burrows to the depth of about 6 inches in mud or hard clay offshore or near salt marshes. Frequently after storms large clumps of old meadow sod or peat are washed ashore from below low tide line, and are found to contain these mollusks. After a storm at Cape May Point, N. J. (September 20, 1928), a log was washed ashore containing a large number of individuals of this species associated with *Pholas truncata* and *Teredo* (Ship Worm).

Known from Prince Edward Island to the Gulf of Mexico, boring in clay or peat.

Tellina tenera Say (Tellen)

PLATE XIV. Fig. 14

A small white shell occasionally tinted pink; common in sand associations from the littoral zone to about 10 fathoms. This species, which is frequently found on the New Jersey beaches, is known from Prince Edward Island to Florida.

Tellina is a southern genus, and many beautiful species are known between Cape Hatteras and Florida and in the West Indies.

Macoma tenta Say

Very similar to the above but without the lateral hinge teeth. Not as common as *T. tenera*, but known from Cape Cod to Florida.

Macoma balthica Linne

PLATE XIV. Fig. 3

A white or pink shell, about an inch long, rounded in shape, often with a thin dusky epidermis; characteristic of brackish water and especially abundant in Delaware Bay.

Known from the Arctic regions, where it is very common, as far south as Georgia.

Macoma calcarea Gmelin

Similar to the above but more pointed posteriorly. A northern species known from the Arctic to

New Jersey; abundant in the north; rare in New Jersey and occasionally found associated with *M. balthica*.

Donax fossor Say (Wedge Clam)

PLATE XIV. Fig. 16

A small shell, up to $\frac{1}{2}$ inch in length, elongated in front, obliquely rounded and short behind. The radiating sculpture is superimposed by a thin layer making the surface of the shell entirely smooth; white or purple in color. Very common on sandy beaches where it often may be seen burrowing into the sand at low tide line just as the waves recede Very common from Long Island to Texas, abundant in New Jersey.

A closely related form, *Donax variabilis* Say is found on beaches from North Carolina southward. This species has the posterior obliquely truncated and the sides noticeably angular; it reaches a length of $1\frac{1}{2}$ inches and usually is more brilliantly colored than the more northern *fossor*. In Florida, where this species is especially abundant, it is known as the Coquina or Pompano Clam, and is often used for broth.

Tagelus gibbus Spengler

PLATE XV. Fig. 2

An elongated white shell covered with a yellowish epidermis. It burrows deep in the mud and is seldom seen alive. The shell is very common on all

New Jersey beaches. Range: Massachusetts to the Gulf of Mexico.

Tagelus divisus Spengler

Smaller and narrower than the above; similar in range and habits, but much rarer.

Ensis directus Conrad (Razor Clam)
(*Solen americana Gould*)

PLATE XV. Fig. 1

This is the common razor clam of the New Jersey coast; shell slightly curved, white, but covered with an olive green epidermis; up to 6 inches in length; two teeth on the right valve and three on the left.

This species is known as the razor clam because of its resemblance to an old fashioned razor. These clams burrow into the mud perpendicularly to a depth of 2 or 3 feet. Sometimes they can be seen projecting slightly out of their holes; however, they burrow very rapidly and are often very difficult to catch.

An easy method of obtaining some of these animals alive is to sprinkle salt on the mud flats where they are living. The salt will cause them to quickly come out of their holes and they may then be readily collected. One must be careful to put the specimens in a jar or other container, because upon being laid flat on the mud they soon recover and with a quick movement of their foot, they may right themselves and burrow rapidly again into the mud.

This clam is common in mud flats and shallow

water from Labrador to Florida and the shell is frequently found on the beach; occasionally used as food.

Ensis viridis Say (Green Razor Clam)

Shell smaller and straighter than the above with a single tooth in each valve; light green in color. Rhode Island to Florida, very rare.

Siliqua costata Say

PLATE XIV. Fig. 12

A very thin elliptical shell, up to 2 inches long; characterized by a rib extending across the inside of the shell; greenish epidermis. Lives in shallow water from Nova Scotia to Cape Hatteras; rare in New Jersey and only occasionally seen on the beach after a storm.

Mactra solidissima Dillwyn (Surf Clam; Sea Clam)

PLATE XIV. Fig. 7, 8

One of the commonest shells on the New Jersey beaches. Shell large, up to 7 inches in length, and covered with a pale brown epidermis which is usually worn off before the shell is washed up on the beach. A triangular shaped cartilage plate at the hinge is characteristic of the family.

Often found living on sandy beaches at low water mark; also dredged in considerable numbers off southern New Jersey from shallow water to 10 fathoms; occasionally used as food, but usually regarded as too tough or too sandy; sometimes gathered in considerable numbers for use as fish bait.

Mulinia lateralis Say (Salt Marsh Clam)
(Mactra lateralis Say)

Fig. 25

Hinge similar to the above but the shell is much smaller (less than an inch in length). A prominent shelf or constriction on the shell is characteristic of this species. Very common in brackish water in sandy associations from 1 to 4 fathoms; especially abundant in Delaware Bay.

Labiosa canaliculata Say

PLATE XVII. Fig. 1

Hinge somewhat similar to *Mactra*, but the shell is very thin and ornamented with ridges; fairly common south of Virginia; broken shells are occasionally found on the beaches of southern New Jersey.

Mesodesma arctatum Conrad
(Ceronia arctata Conrad)

PLATE XIV. Fig. 15

A northern species that is occasionally found on the New Jersey beaches from Seaside Park northward.

Mya arenaria Linne (Soft Shelled Clam; Nanny-Nose)

PLATE XIX. Fig. 6

Shell oval and not as thick as the Hard Shell Clam (*Venus*). A single large tooth on one valve fits into a pit on the opposite valve.

The soft clam lives in mud flats along the New Jersey coast, but usually prefers a more muddy association than *Venus*. Its siphons are much longer than those of the hard clam and may even be longer than the shell of the clam. When disturbed in its burrow it quickly withdraws its siphon within the shell ejecting a jet of water into the air. Its usual size is 2 to 3 inches in length. Known from the Arctic regions to Cape Hatteras, but rare south of Chesapeake Bay. It is used as food, but is not quite as popular in New Jersey as the Hard Shell Clam.

Corbula contracta Say

PLATE XIX. Fig. 8

About half an inch long with a single tooth in each valve fitting into a pit on the opposite valve; shell smooth with concentric ridges. Cape Cod to Florida; occasionally dredged in shallow water off the New Jersey coast.

PLATE XVII.

1. **Labiosa canaliculata** Say 2. **Pholas costata** Linne
3. **Pecten grandis** Solander

Pholas costata Linne

(*Barnea costata Linne*) (Large Angel Wings)

PLATE XVII. Fig. 2

This conspicuous white shell reaches as much as 6 inches in length. It burrows 2 feet or more deep in the mud or clay and is very difficult to obtain alive. This species had not been seen alive along our northeastern coast for a good many years and it was thought that they were possibly becoming extinct. However, it has recently turned up again and is found to live in considerable numbers in the mud flats along Delaware Bay and in Cape May Harbor.

There is a large bed of these mollusks along Delaware Bay near Fishing Creek. They can sometimes be seen at low tide in the shallow pools with their siphons slightly elevated above the mud. Upon trying to capture them, they burrow very rapidly some two feet or more into the mud. In attempting to resist capture the animal will frequently draw itself into the shell with such force that the shell becomes broken. The shell is indeed very fragile and although many fragments are found on the New Jersey beaches, it is seldom than one finds a perfect pair.

A few years ago a fisherman at Cape May found a bed of these bivalves in Cape May Harbor and reported that they were good to eat.

These shells are known from Cape Cod to the West Indies, and are more frequent on beaches south of Cape Hatteras.

Although not closely related, this shell at first glance resembles *Petricola pholadiformis* and the popular name for the two species is sometimes the same.

Pholas truncata Say
(*Barnea truncata Say*)

PLATE XV. Fig. 5

Smaller than the above and more truncate; burrows in mud and peat and found between Maine and the Gulf of Mexico. The shell is fairly common in New Jersey, especially along Delaware Bay beaches; it has been observed burrowing into a log washed ashore at Cape May Point. (September 21, 1928).

Zirphaea crispata Linne

Somewhat similar in general appearance to the above but with a prominent furrow which divided each valve into two parts.

A northern shell living in hard clay or rocks; very rare in New Jersey.

Teredo navalis Linne (Ship Worm)

Fig. 26

One would naturally expect that the ship worm was an annelid worm. However, it is really a bivalve mollusk of a very modified type. It is wormlike in form and lives in a shelly tube not unlike that of the worm *Eupomotus dianthus*. It does however, have a very small shell (1/4 inch long) at the wider end of the tube. At the other end of the tube there are two calcareous structures known as pallets which are used to close the tube.

Ship worms bore into submerged wood and are

Fig. 26

Wood bored by Shipworm (Teredo navallis Linne)

very destructive to piling, wharves, buoys and even vessels. Various kinds of paints have been perfected to coat the wood in an attempt to protect it from the ravages of this pest.

The ship worm is world-wide in distribution; along the New Jersey coast the tubes grow to 6 inches in length. In tropical waters they may attain the length of two feet or more.

Various species or varieties of the ship worm have been described, based upon slight differences in the shell or pallets.

GASTROPODA

The word Gastropoda means stomach-footed; the foot of this mollusk is really a thickening of the surface of the animal, giving the impression that the animal walks on its stomach. There is a great deal of variation in the size and shape of the foot among the various species of gastropods.

As contrasted to the bivalves, the gastropods are often called univalves because they usually possess a single shell, generally coiled or spiral; a few, however, such as the slugs and nudibranchs possess no external shell whatever. (These are not treated in this book.)

Another common name for this group of mollusks is Sea Snails.

The opening through which the animal projects out of the shell is known as the aperture and is in some species covered by a horny or calcareous lid known as the operculum.

The top of the shell is called the apex and each turn of the spiral is known as a whorl. The sculpture of the whorls is often very complicated and is of importance in the determination of the various species. The outer edge of the aperture is known as the outer lip, while the inner lip is termed the columella.

Although externally very different from the bivalves, the internal anatomy of both bivalves and univalves is essentially similar. One structure, however, peculiar to univalves is the radula or tongue. This structure is equipped with many small teeth and is used to grind the food obtained by the mollusk. The radula is hidden among the muscular tissue which lines the inside of the snail. The structure of the radula is of great importance in the differentiation of species, particularly of land mollusks.

As is the case with the Pelecypoda many gastropods are of economic importance as food, although they seem not to be especially favored along our coast. Among others, the Moon Snail (*Polinices heros*) and the Periwinkle (*Littorina litorea*) are eaten with much relish in Newfoundland, and various species of Conch (*Strombus, Fulgur*, etc.) are often eaten in Florida and the West Indies.

Gastropods are found in the sea, in fresh water and on land.

Fissurella alternata Say (Key Hole Limpet)

Fig. 30 B

A southern shell occasionally found on the beaches of southern New Jersey, probably washed from a Pleistocene fossil deposit. Not known alive north of Cape Hatteras.

Scalaria lineata Say
(*Scala lineata Say; Epitonium lineatum (Say)*)

Fig. 30 D

Shell white, sometimes with a few brown lines; about 1 inch long with about eight whorls, prominently ribbed. Not common on the beach, but occasionally found in from 2 to 25 fathoms off shore; known from Vineyard Sound to the Gulf of Mexico; more common north of New Jersey.

Scalaria humphrysii Kiener
(*Scalaria sayana Dall; Epitonium humphrysii (Kiener)*)

PLATE XX. Fig. 11

Ribs more prominent than those of the above; color usually pure white; similar in habits and range as the above; rare.

Janthina janthina Linne (Floating Shell)
(J. communis Lamarck; J. fragilis Lamarck)

Fig. 27

A pelagic species, that is one that floats on the surface of the sea, usually far from shore. After storms they are occasionally washed upon the beaches from Nantucket to the West Indies. The shell is very thin and is usually purple in color. The animal is kept on the surface of the water by a gelatinous secretion from the foot. Very rare on New Jersey beaches (one record from Cape May Point); more common on Florida beaches.

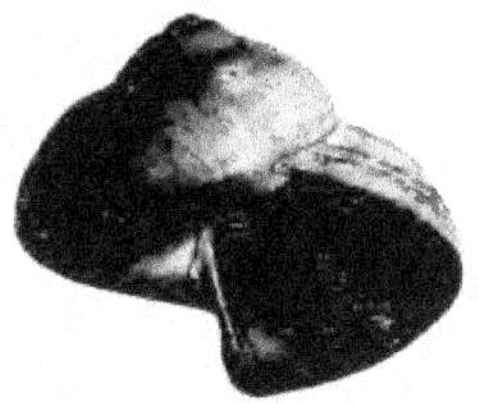

Fig. 27

Janthina janthina Linne

Stilifer stimpsoni Verrill

A small, elongate shell that lives among the spines of the Green Sea Urchin (*Strongylocentrotus drobachiensis*), usually in deep water. One record from 35 fathoms off New Jersey.

PLATE XVIII

1. Crepidula fornicata Linne
2. Crepidula plana Say
3. Sinum perspectivum Say
4. Crepidula convexa Say
5. Columbella avara Say
6. Nassa trivittata Say
7. Melampus li[illegible]atus Say
8. Terebra c[illegible]va Say
9. " "
10. Terebra [illegible]ocata Say
11. Polinices duplicata Say
12. Polinices heros Say

PLATE XVIII.

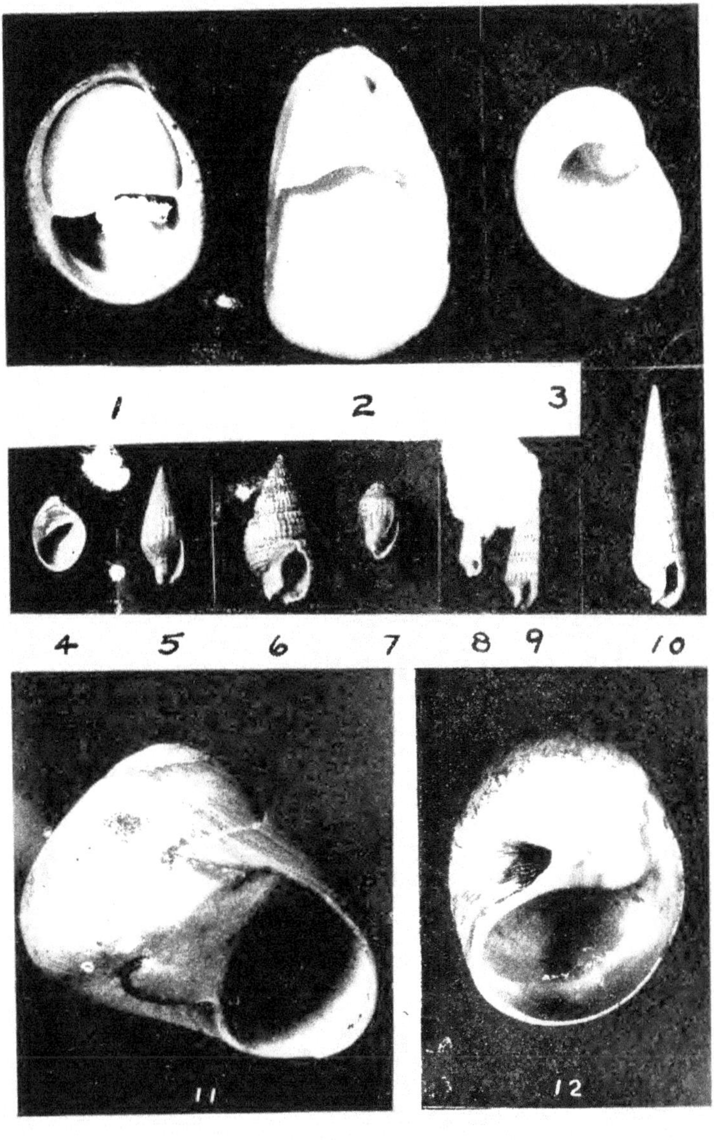

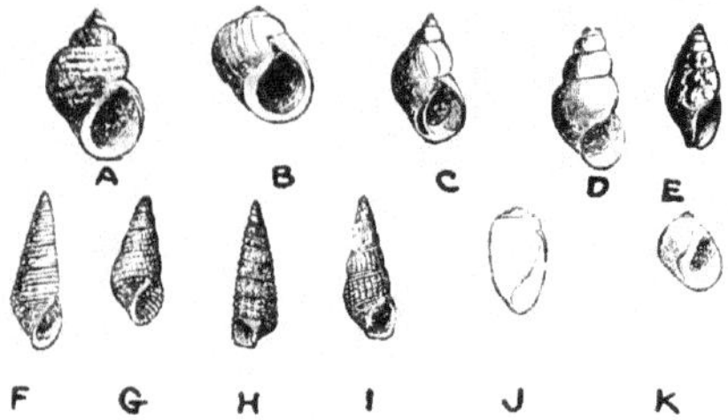

Fig. 28

(a) Littorina saxatila; (b) L. obtussata; (c) Lacuna vincta; (d) Paludestrina minuta; (e) Columbella lunata; (f) Odostomia impressa; (g) O. seminuda; (h) Triphora perversa nigrocincta; (i) Bittium alternatum; (j) Actoocina canaliculata; (k) Natica pusila.

Odostomia impressa Say

Fig. 28 F

A small smooth shell (less than ¼ inch long) occasionally found on sea weed between the tides and in shallow water.

Odostomia seminuda C. B. Adams

Fig. 28 G

Similar in general appearance and habits to the above, but distinguished by its more granulated surface.

Turbonilla

This is a genus composed of numerous species of minute shells, several of which are to be found in New Jersey waters. They are long, slender spiral shells, seldom reaching ½ inch in length. The various species are very difficult to determine. They can be distinguished from *Odostomia* by an oblique fold on the columella (shell axis).

The most common New Jersey species are *T. conradi* Bush and *T. interrupta* Totten.

Fig. 29
Polinices duplicata Say

Polinices duplicata Say (*Natica duplicata Say*) (Sea Snail; Moon Snail; Sand Collar Snail)

PLATE XVIII. Fig. 11; Fig. 29

A large shell (up to 3 inches in diameter) with a comparatively flat apex; characterized by a thick brown callus almost covering the umbilicus. Usually found partially buried in the sand from the intertidal zone to relatively deep water; known from Massachusetts to the Gulf of Mexico; common in New Jersey.

This snail forms a curious egg case known as the sand collar. The animal glues together grains of sand in the form of a collar and deposits its eggs in the gelatinous substance between the sand grains. (Fig. 29) The operculum (or lid of the shell) is horny.

Polinices heros Say (Moon Snail)

PLATE XVIII. Fig. 12

Somewhat similar to the above but without the callus on the umbilicus; therefore easily distinguished by the "hole". Often larger than *duplicata* (up to 4 inches); similar habits as the above but more common in deeper water (to 238 fathoms). Found between Newfoundland and North Carolina, especially abundant north of Long Island Sound. Used as bait for cod fish.

Polinices triseriata Say

Exactly similar to *P. heros* except for its smaller size and for three rows of brown spots on the shell; probably the young of *P. heros*.

Natica pusila Say

Fig. 28 K

Shell small (1/4 inch) with white callus almost completely filling the umbilicus. Lives in shallow water from Massachusetts to Florida. Not common in New Jersey coastal waters but occasionally dredged off shore.

Natica clausa Broderip and Sowerby

A small species with a white callus in the umbilicus; operculum (lid) calcareous instead of horny (as in *heros, triseriata* and *duplicata*). A northern species very rare in New Jersey.

Sinum perspectivum Say (Ear Shell)
(*Sigaretus perspectivus Say*)

PLATE XVIII. Fig. 3

A flat ear-shaped shell which is really a modified *Natica*. Common on southern beaches but only a few have been found in New Jersey (Atlantic City, Wildwood, Two Mile Beach and Cape May); some of these may be fossils.

Crepidula fornicata Linne (Boat Shell; Slipper Limpet)

PLATE XVIII. Fig. 1

One of the most easily recognized shells of the New Jersey beaches. The top of the shell is pointed and the spire is merely an inconspicuous apex closely pressed against the shell. The top part of the shell is rounded giving it a boat-like appearance. A shelf covering the upper part of the aperture

PLATE XIX

1. **Fulgur canaliculata** Linne
2. **Fulgur perversa** Linne
3. **Fulgur carica** Gmelin
4. **Cyprina islandica** Linne
5. **Venus mercenaria** Linne
6. **Mya arenaria** Linne
7. **Marginella guttata** Dillwyn
8. **Corbula contracta** Say
9. **Venericardia tridentata** Say
10. **Modiolus demissus** Dillwyn
11. **Modiolus modiolus** Linne
12. **Mytilus recurvus** Rafinesque

PLATE XIX.

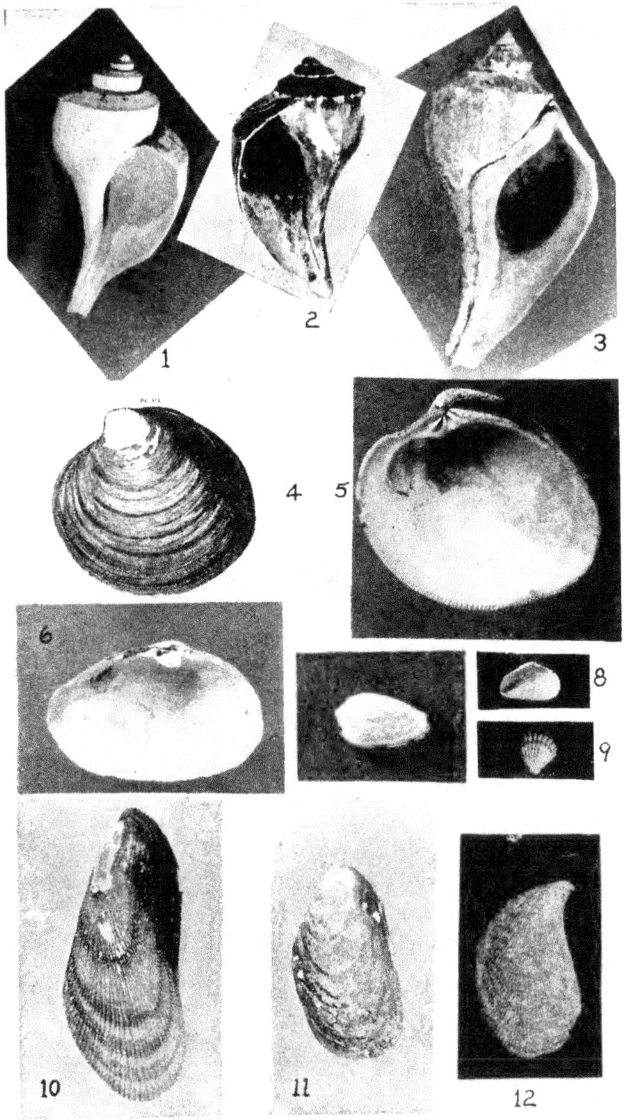

corresponds to the forecastle of the ship. The color is white frequently with brown markings.

These shells are found attached to other shells, stones, and often to each other; most frequent on shells inhabited by hermit crabs. Very large boat shells are sometimes found attached to King Crabs and occasionally to Blue Crabs.

Variable in shape because of the object to which they are attached. Very common all along the New Jersey coast from tide pools to at least 25 fathoms; range: Prince Edward Island to the West Indies.

Crepidula plana Say (Flat Boat Shell; White Boat Shell)

PLATE XVIII. Fig. 2

Shell white and flat with suppressed spire at the tip of the "bow"; The "stern" is square. Found on the inside of shells, frequently those inhabited by Hermit Crabs; occasionally on the outside of flat shells, such as the oyster. Similar distribution to the above.

Crepidula convexa Say (Convex Boat Shell)

PLATE XVIII. Fig. 4

Very convex; usually spotted brown in color; grows on pebbles or other objects suitable to its shape. Very abundant from Nova Scotia to Florida.

Paludestrina minuta Totten
(*Rissoa minuta Totten*)

Fig. 28 D

A small (1/4 inch) shell common in salt marsh pools and brackish waters from James Bay and Labrador to New Jersey; often found on sea weed in New Jersey Inland Waterways. It can often be obtained by drying masses of Sea Lettuce (*Ulva*) and then shaking it thoroughly and collecting the small shells that were adhering to it.

Littorina litorea Linne (Periwinkle; Wrinkle)

PLATE XX. Fig. 6

This thick black shell is the most conspicuous member of the littoral marine fauna from Labrador to Long Island. It is said to have been accidently introduced into Nova Scotia from the Old World about 1863 and has since migrated north and south along the coast. It is usually associated with a rocky coast and is therefore not to be expected along the sandy shores of New Jersey. However, the rock breakwaters along the coast have in recent years afforded a habitat for this species and it is now firmly established at a number of places along the New Jersey coast. As far as is known, Cape May is the southermost point that the Periwinkle has yet been reported.

In Great Britain and other European countries these periwinkles are used as food and are regarded as quite a delicacy. In Newfoundland, where they are known as "Wrinkles" they are also frequently eaten.

Littorina irrorata Say (Salt Marsh Periwinkle)

PLATE XX. Fig. 4

Resembles *L. litorea* in general appearance but with a higher spire; usually white with a series of brown revolving lines or dots. Very common in New Jersey attached to Eel Grass or other salt marsh plants. It is usually found between tides or above high tide and lives in brackish or even almost fresh water. Known from Massachusetts to Texas, but is rare north of New Jersey and possibly in some cases a recent addition either by migration or introduction with oysters.

Littorina obtusata Linne
(*L. paliata Say*)

Fig. 28 B

Small (½ inch in length), low spired, usually olive in color, occasionally banded. Found on sea weed and associated with *L. litorea* along the coast of New England. Rare in New Jersey but occasionally found in brackish water or associated with *L. litorea* on various rock jetties along the coast. Cape May appears to be its southern limit.

Littorina saxatila Olivi
(*L. rudis Maton; L. groenlandica Menke*)

Fig. 28 A

About the same size as the above; the spire is higher and there are usually revolving bands; usually white or olive in color. Similar habits as *L. obtussata*; known from Cape May, N. J. to Labrador and Hudson Bay.

Lacuna vincta Montagu

Fig. 28 C

Shell less than ½ inch in length, usually purplish in color. The umbilicus forms a lengthened groove along the columella. A northern shell known from Labrador to New Jersey. It is frequently common on Sea Lettuce (*Ulva*) between the tides and in shallow water. It is inconspicuous on the living sea weed, and may best be found by drying some, and then shaking it to obtain the small shells that were adhering to the weed; often associated with *Paludestrina minuta*. Cape May is the southern limit.

Cerithiopsis subulata Montagu
(*C. emersoni Adams*)

PLATE XX. Fig. 9

A small gastropod known from 2 to 15 fathoms between Massachusetts and the West Indies. Not seen alive in New Jersey waters, but occasionally found in the Pleistocene deposits or washed upon the beach.

Triphora perversa nigrocincta C. B. Adams

Fig. 28 H

Shell black, about ½ inch long. This species is easily recognized because it is sinistral or left-handed—that is the whorls turn to the left and the opening is on the left side. Cape Cod to Florida; rare in New Jersey.

Bittium alternatum Say
(*B. nigrum Totten; Diastoma virginica Henderson & Bartsch*

PLATE XX. Fig. 10

A right handed shell about ½ inch long; rounded aperture; often abundant in shallow water Massachusetts to North Carolina.

Urosalpinx cinerea Say (Oyster Drill; Drill; Borer)

PLATE XX. Fig. 8

These gastropods bore small round holes in shells, particularly those of the young oyster. They are found in great numbers in Delaware Bay where they cause considerable damage to the beds in Maurice River Cove. They are especially abundant below low tide, although they may sometimes be seen alive on the exposed beach or mud flats. They are not as resistant to fresh water as the oyster and are therefore not common in the upper part of Delaware Bay and are rare above Fortesque. Drills are also common along the rest of the New Jersey coast. The species is known from Prince Edward Island to Florida, and is particularly abundant in Long Island Sound, Delaware Bay and Chesapeake Bay where it feeds on young oysters.

Eupleura caudata Say (Oyster Drill; Drill; Borer)

Fig. 30 C

Flatter in appearance than *Urosalpinx* but similar to it in habits and distribution, although not nearly as common. Of some 10,000 borers taken from Delaware Bay by the New Jersey Oyster Investigation Laboratory in one season, 3% proved to be this species, the other 97% being *Urosalpinx*.

Thais floridana Conrad

(*Purpura haemastoma floridana Conrad*)

PLATE XX. Fig. 7

Although not known alive north of North Carolina, the shell is occasionally found on New Jersey beaches where they have probably been washed from some fossil deposit.

In southern waters where this species abounds, they cause considerable damage to oysters by drilling holes in the same manner as *Urosalpinx* and *Eupleura*.

PLATE XX

1. **Buccinum undatum** Linne
.. **Colus gracilis** Da Costa
3. **Neptunea stonei** Pilsbry
4. **Littorina irrorata** Say
5. **Nassa vibex** Say
6. **Littorina litorea** Linne
7. **Thais floridana** Conrad
8. **Urosalpinx cinerea** Say
9. **Cerithiopsis subulata** Montagu
10. **Bittium alternatum** Say
11. **Scalaria humphrysii** Kiener

PLATE XX.

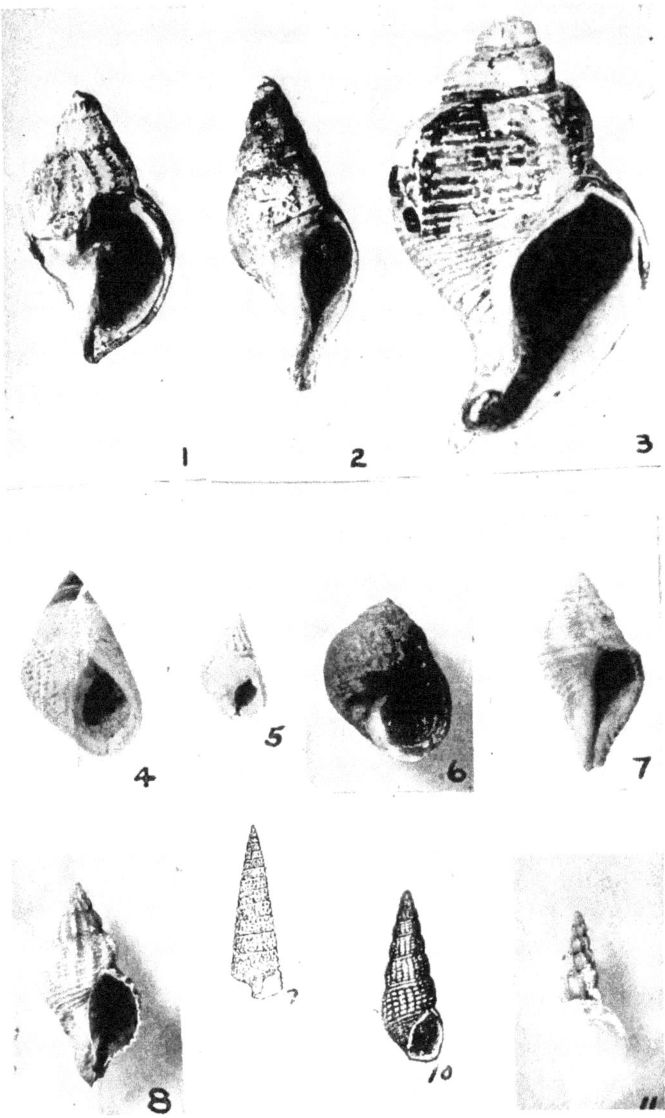

Columbella avara Say
(*Anachis avara Say*)

PLATE XVIII, Fig. 5

A slender shell about ½ inch long; upper whorls smooth, lower ones undulated; yellowish white in color. Fairly common in sandy associations from 3 to 25 fathoms; not found in the intertidal zone or in the inland waterways. Known from Massachusetts to Florida.

Columbella lunata Say
(*Mitrella lunata Say; Astyris lunata Say*)

Fig. 28 E

Less than ¼ inch in length; reddish brown with circular rows of white spots or "half moons". Common on sea weed, etc. from low tide to 10 fathoms or more, particularly abundant on the bryozoon *Bugula turrita* in a large area of 3 to 6 fathoms depth off Wildwood and Cape May.

Nassa obsoleta Say (Mud Snail)
(*Nassarius obsoleta Say; Alectrion obsoleta Say*)

Fig. 30 A

This small (1 inch) black snail is exceedingly abundant on mud flats from between the tides to about 2 fathoms, occasionally deeper; usually found in inlets or in brackish water, never in the open ocean; the mud flats along Delaware Bay are almost

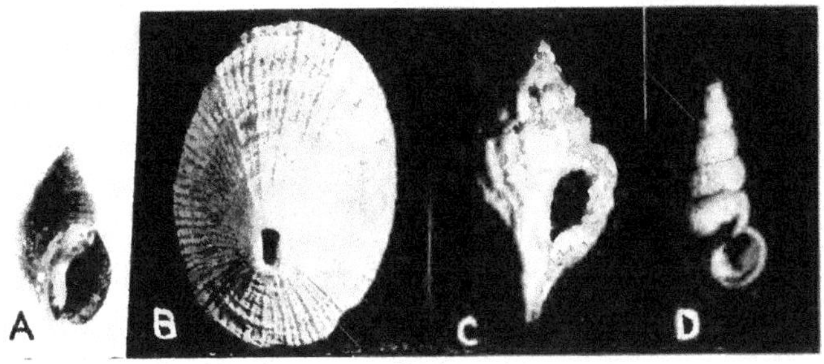

Fig. 30
(a) Nassa obsoleta; (b) Fissurella alternata; (c) Eupleura caudata; (d) Scalaria lineata

literally covered with these snails. This species does not drill holes in oyster shells as does *Urosalpinx* and *Eupleura* but is a scavenger and eagerly devours dead animals of various kinds.

The eggs, small white bodies, are common in May and June and may be found attached to sea weeds or floating plants. The species is known from the Gulf of St. Lawrence to Florida; the mud flats of New Jersey are perhaps its favorite home.

Nassa trivittata Say (Sand Flat Snail; White Mud Snail)

(*Nassarius trivittata Say; Tritia trivittata Say; Alectrion trivittata Say*)

PLATE XVIII. Fig. 6

About the size of *N. obsoleta*, but white and granulated in appearance. Common on sandy shores from just below low tide to fathoms; more common in the open ocean than in the inlets and bays although it is frequent in parts of Delaware Bay. Shells of this and the above species, often inhabited by Hermit Crabs are very abundant in tide pools and washed up on the beaches. Known from the Gulf of St. Lawrence to Florida.

Nassa vibex Say (Southern Mud Snail)

PLATE XX. Fig. 5

This species is not common north of Cape Charles, Virginia. It has, however, been collected alive from the New Jersey coast and as far north as Vineyard Sound, Massachusetts. The shell is slightly smaller than the two preceding species and is white with brownish spots. It is very common in sandy bays along the Florida coast; known from the Pleistocene deposits of New Jersey.

Fig. 31

Neptunea decemcostata Say

Buccinum undatum Linne (Whelk)

PLATE XX. Fig. 1

This large gastropod (2 to 3 inches long) is common on the coast of Newfoundland and along northern New England. Farther south it is restricted to deep water and off New Jersey is known only from 32 fathoms or deeper. Occasionally shells are found on the beach, some of which are probably fossils which lived during a part of the Pleistocene when the climate was cooler than the present—probably during a glacial stage.

The peculiar egg masses of this species are common on northern beaches and are occasionally dredged in deep water off New Jersey or as far south as Ocean City, Maryland, the recorded southern limit of the species.

Neptunea decemcostata Say

Fig. 31

A large shell decorated with ten revolving ribs; known from Nova Scotia to Massachusetts Bay. A few fossil specimens have been found on the New Jersey beaches; these, like the above species probably lived off the New Jersey coast during Glacial times when the water was considerably cooler than it is to-day.

Neptunea stonei Pilsbry

(*Chrysodomus stonei Pilsbry*)

PLATE XX. Fig. 3

An extinct species that is occasionally picked up on the New Jersey beaches. It is known from Pleistocene deposits on Gardiners Island, N. Y., Marthas Vineyard and Nantucket, Massachusetts, and probably lived during or just before the last glaciation; rare and never found perfect.

Colus gracilis DaCosta

PLATE XX. Fig. 2

Another northern species which probably lived in New Jersey waters during the Glacial period; one fossil shell has been found on the beach at Asbury Park, N. J.

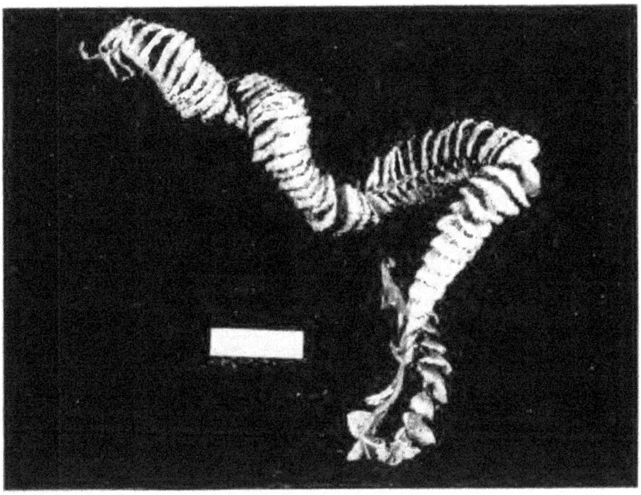

Fig. 32
Egg case of Conch **(Fulgur)**

Fulgur carica Gmelin (Knobbed Conch)
(*Busycon caricum Gmelin*)

PLATE XIX. Fig. 3

The conchs are the largest gastropod shells north of Cape Hatteras. They may be seen crawling among the Eel Grass in shallow water or may be dredged from deep water; the shells are common on most beaches. The conch has a proboscis like an elephant's trunk, which it holds before it as it crawls about looking for food.

The Knobbed Conch is the largest of the Conchs off the coast of New Jersey and adjacent states and may reach 9 inches in length. It may easily be identified by the wart-like knobs near the top of the shell.

This conch as well as the two following species, is edible, but it is not extensively used along this coast.

The egg cases of this species are often found upon the beach (Figure 32). If one of the pockets of a mature case is opened, one will discover scores of minute "baby conch shells."

Known from Cape Cod to Florida.

Fulgur canaliculata Linne (Channeled Conch)
(*Busycon canaliculatum Linne.*)

PLATE XIX., Fig. 1

This specie [illegible] ..ghtly smaller than the above conch; instead of having knobs, the shoulder is flattened and there are deeply channeled sutures. Same distribution as the above. The egg case of this species differs from the above in that the margins of the capsules or pockets are thin and wedge-shaped rather than square and angular.

Fulgur perversa Linne (Left-Handed Conch)
(Busycon perversum Linne)

PLATE XIX. Fig. 2

Similar to the above species except that it is sinistral or "left-handed." In other words the opening is on the left instead of the right as in *carica* and *canaliculata*. For this reason most people call it the "left-handed conch." However, according to some, this is a "right-handed" shell, whereas the other two species are "left-handed," because *perversa* is held in the *right* hand when used as a drinking cup and the other species are held in the *left* hand. This double meaning of the popular name has caused some rather amusing incidents among collectors.

F. perversa is not known alive to-day north of Cape Hatteras. Nevertheless worn shells are occasionally found on the beaches as far north as New Jersey and occasionally southern New England. It is believed that these are fossil shells and that they were washed from some deposit of Pleistocene age. This species apparently lived in New Jersey waters during interglacial time, when the climate was somewhat milder than that of the present.

Marginella guttata Dillwyn

PLATE XIX. Fig. 7

An attractive southern shell that has only recently been found in New Jersey waters; about an inch long and usually pink in color.

Terebra dislocata Say (Spiral; Staircase Shell)

PLATE XVIII. Fig. 10

A spiral shell up to 2 inches long; numerous minute radiating lines; prominently ribbed with numerous revolving grooves.

Although this species is not known alive north of North Carolina (or possibly Maryland), shells are occasionally found on the New Jersey beaches. The species is frequent in the Pleistocene (interglacial) deposits and it is probable that the beach shells were transported from some such deposit.

Terebra concava Say

PLATE XVIII. Fig. 8, 9

Distinguished from the above because the radiating lines or nodules do not extend across the grooves. Similar distribution as *T. dislocata* but not quite as common in the Pleistocene of New Jersey.

Mangelia cerina Kurtz and Stimpson

This small species, although reported from Massachusetts to Florida in 3 to 10 fathoms, has not been found alive in New Jersey waters; known from the Pleistocene (interglacial) deposits at Two Mile Beach.

Mangelia plicosa C. B. Adams

Range similar to that of the above; not found alive in New Jersey although present in the Pleistocene (interglacial) deposits at Two Mile Beach and Peermont.

Acteocina canaliculata Say
(*Tornatina canaliculata Say*)

Fig. 28 J

A small (1/4 inch) white shell occasionally found on sea weed or dredged in shallow water between Prince Edward Island and Florida.

Melampus lineatus Say (Salt Marsh Snail;
(*M. bidentatus Montagu*) Coffee Snail)

PLATE XVIII. Fig. 7

A small brown pulmonate (air breathing) snail that is always found near salt water; almost always found above high tide line; since, contrary to most marine snails, it is air breathing, it seldom is found in the water, although it has been found on some mussels (*Mytilus edulis*) submerged between the tides.

CEPHALOPODA

The name Cephalopoda means head-footed and was applied to this group of mollusks, because the foot is partly fused with the head above the eyes and around the mouth.

Except for the *Nautilus* and one or two others, the animals of this group do not possess an external shell. The shell is internal and very much modified. The common squid (*Loligo pealei*) has a horny structure known as the pen which is really a modified internal shell. The Squid of the Mediterranean (*Sepia*) has a hard pen known as the cuttle bone, of which the canary birds are so fond.

In former geological ages, Cephalopods were much more abundant than at present and their fossil remains are often abundant in the rocks. Many reached a great size, either elongate such as the modern squid, or coiled like the Nautilus. Pens of *Bellemnitella americana* are abundant in the Cretaceous deposits of New Jersey and elsewhere on the Southern Atlantic Coastal Plain.

Loligo pealei Leseur (Squid)

Fig. 33

Body cylindrical, about 8 inches long, tapering to a point; terminal fins about half as long as the body. The internal shell or pen is as long as the main part of the animal; conspicuous eyes equipped with a cornea.

The squid resembles a submarine boat. Its method of locomotion is rather unique. It squirts a stream of water from a little tube near its neck; if it squirts forward, the animal moves backward. The squid, therefore, is the Rocket Animal of the

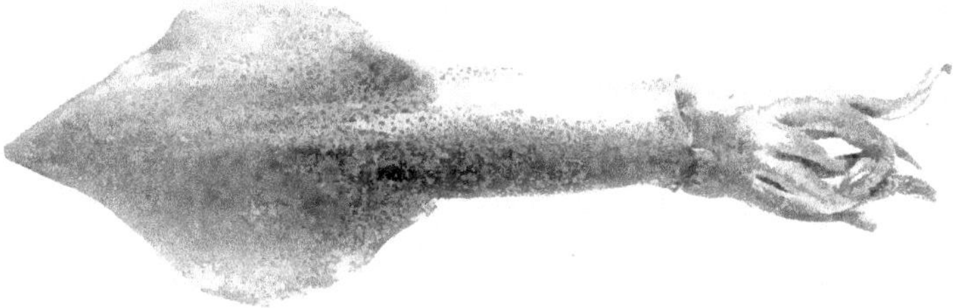

Fig. 33
Loligo pealei Leseur

sea. It can move just as rapidly in either direction.

The pen acts as a sort of backbone to support the soft parts of the body. This pen is really the shell of the animal, which has become very much modified and is entirely within the body of the animal.

If the squid is in danger, it will discharge a great quantity of a black fluid out of its mouth, which acts like a smoke screen and enables it to escape. This fluid is India ink.

The squid is often caught off the New Jersey coast for use as bait. It is usually found in the open ocean and rarely comes within a mile or so of shore.

Its eggs are laid in elongate jelly-like masses about 3 inches long which form large clusters on stones or other submerged objects. Thousands of minute squid can sometimes be seen in one of these masses which occasionally wash ashore in the early summer.

In some countries the squid is considered quite a delicacy, but it is seldom eaten in the United States.

Ommastrephes illecebrosus Lesueur (Sea Arrow; Flying Squid)

Similar to the above but with fins only half as long as the trunk and with eyes not equipped with a cornea. A more northern species which usually lives farther from shore than *Loligo*. Known from New Jersey to the Bay of Fundy.

Rossia sublaevis Verrill

About 2 inches in length with fins near the middle of the body; pen small.

A northern species not hitherto reported south of Cape Cod. Occasionally seen in New Jersey waters especially during the winter.

Octopus sp. (Octopus)

The octopus has been reported from New Jersey waters but its presence has not been verified. It resembles a squid but has a much larger head, proportionally, and possesses eight arms which are equipped with suckers.

The terrifying stories about the tropical octopus do not apply to those individuals from New Jersey and vicinity. If it does occur in New Jersey, the specimens would be small and entirely harmless and might easily be confused with the common Squid.

CHAPTER TWELVE

CRUSTACEA

1. COPEPODA (Copepods)
2. CIRRIPEDIA (Barnacles)
3. MYSIDACEA (Mysids; Opossum Shrimp)
4. EUPHAUSIACEA (Euphausids)
5. AMPHIPODA (Amphipods; Beach Fleas; Scuds; etc.)
6. ISOPODA (Isopods)
7. STOMATOPODA (Squill)
8. DECAPODA (Shrimps, Lobsters, Crabs, etc.)

COPEPODA
(Copepods)

To this group belong a great many very minute forms which are of great importance because they form a large part of the food of many fishes. Many copepods live on the surface of the sea and may be collected by means of a "tow net" or "plankton net," usually made of fine silk or bolting cloth to the end of which is attached a small bottle. This net is dragged behind a slowly moving boat and these minute creatures are gathered by the net and concentrated in the bottle. Small jellyfish and other plankton or floating animals are obtained in the same way. Many more species of copepods live in the sand along beaches and off-shore bars.

In addition to the great many free living copepods, there are numerous species that are parasitic on fishes and other sea animals.

The copepods are too minute to be seen by the

average collector, or if seen the species are very difficult to determine. Therefore they are not treated in this book.

Other minute Crustacea often obtained by a tow net, which are not discussed in this book, are the Cladocera (Water fleas), Ostracoda and Cumacea.

CIRRIPEDIA
(Barnacles)

Barnacles were for a long time classified with the Mollusca (shell-fish) and it was not until their life history was studied that their position within the group Crustacea was fully recognized.

When young, the barnacle is a minute free-swimming animal with one eye, three pairs of legs and a single shell. It grows and moults in the manner of an insect until it has two eyes, six pairs of legs and two shells. Then it attaches itself to some solid object and completely changes its appearance. The bivalve shell disappears and it develops a new shell made up of various plates. The legs become modified to "cirripeds"—meaning curled legs—giving the name to the order. These legs are feather-like and, when extended, are constantly waving, thus creating a current which carries food to the mouth of the barnacle. These legs are withdrawn within the shell when the animal is disturbed.

Some barnacles are sessile, attaching themselves directly to some solid object; others are stalked. Many barnacles attach themselves to ships and often occur in such great numbers as seriously to diminish the speed of the vessel.

Lepas anatifera Linne (Goose Barnacle)

PLATE XXI.

On fleshy stalk which is about as long as the shell of the barnacle (1 inch); shell smooth and white. Attaches to ships, driftwood, etc., and is of worldwide distribution. Periodic along the New Jersey coast and when present is apt to be exceedingly abundant, for example, late in the summer of 1931 when the Jersey beaches were covered with driftwood to which this barnacle was attached.

There is an old tradition that these shells, which somewhat resemble eggs, hatched into geese—hence the common name Goose Barnacle.

Balanus balanoides Linne (Rock Barnacle)

PLATE XXII.

Very common on rocks between the tides; grows abundantly on the rocky coast of New England; south of Long Island it is found only where rock jetties have been built; it is attached to the rock by its membraneous base, known as far south as Cape Charles, Virginia.

Balanus eburneus Gould (Ivory Barnacle)

PLATE XXIII.

Found at or below low tide, especially on woodwork; frequently found inside large shells and occasionally on the back of King Crabs; young barnacles are sometimes found on sea weed; easily

PLATE XXI.

Lepas anatifera Linne

distinguished from the above by its shelly base. Range: Massachusetts to South America in shallow water; extends into brackish and almost fresh water.

Balanus crenatus Bruguiere

A white barnacle, usually rougher in appearance than *B. eburneus* and with a somewhat thinner calcareous base; about 1 inch wide and up to 1½ inches high, although usually less.

Common on rocks and stones from Long Island Sound northward; rare in New Jersey, although occasionally found as far south as Cape May.

Balanus amphitrite niveus Darwin

Resembles *B. crenatus* with which it may easily be confused; it may, however, be differentiated by its smaller size and by the fact that its base is porous, whereas in *crenatus* it is not, and also by the fact that there is a fairly well marked ridge on the scutum (plate of the shell). Rarely reaches more than ½ inch in diameter.

Grows on wood etc. from Cape Cod to Florida. Not common in New Jersey.

Chelonobia testudinaria Linne (Turtle Barnacle)

Fig. 34

A large white barnacle that lives attached to the shells of Sea Turtles.

PLATE XXII.

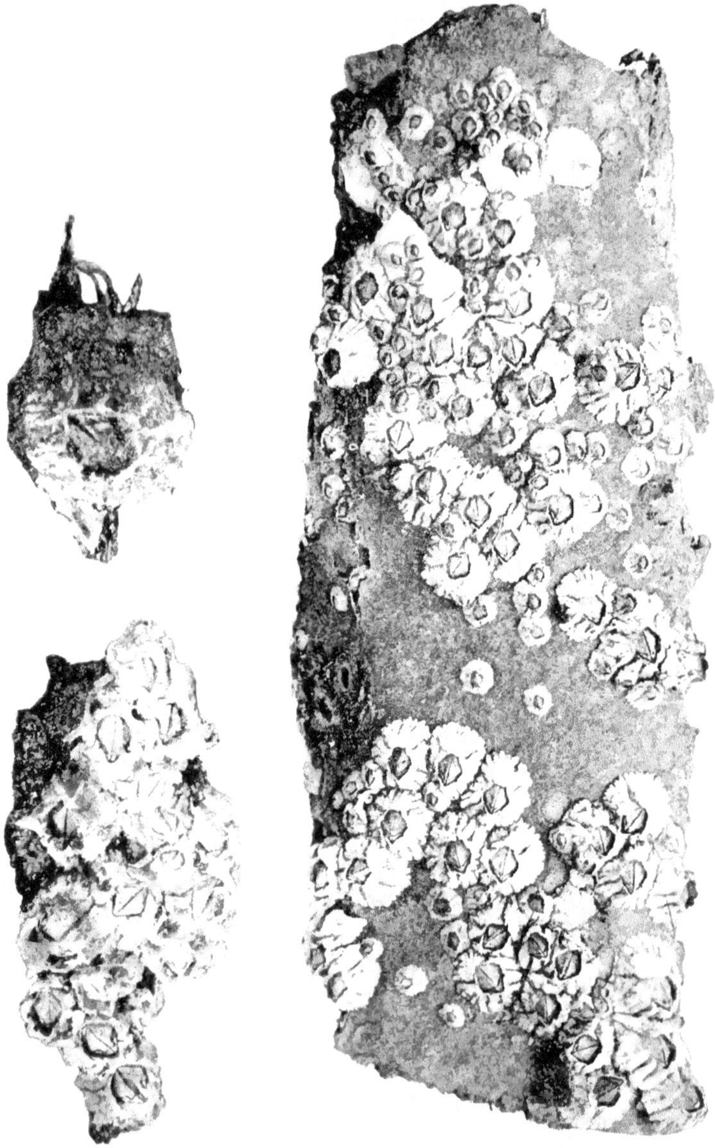

Balanus balanoides Linne

Balanus eburneus Gould

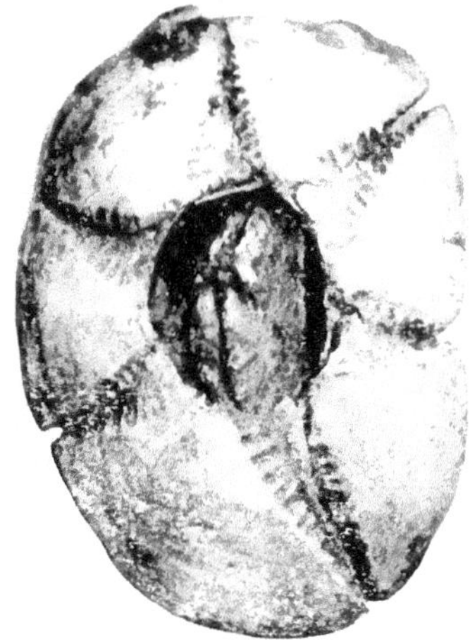

Fig. 34

Chelonobia testudinoria Linne

Platylepas hexastylos Fabricius

Fig. 35

Lives on the Green Turtle (*Chelonia mydas* Linne). Noted at Cape May, New Jersey and Chincoteague, Virginia.

Coronula diadema Linne (Whale Barnacle)

Fig. 36

A crown-shaped barnacle that attaches itself to the back of whales; known in New Jersey from whales off Sandy Hook and from a broken piece washed on the beach at Cape May.

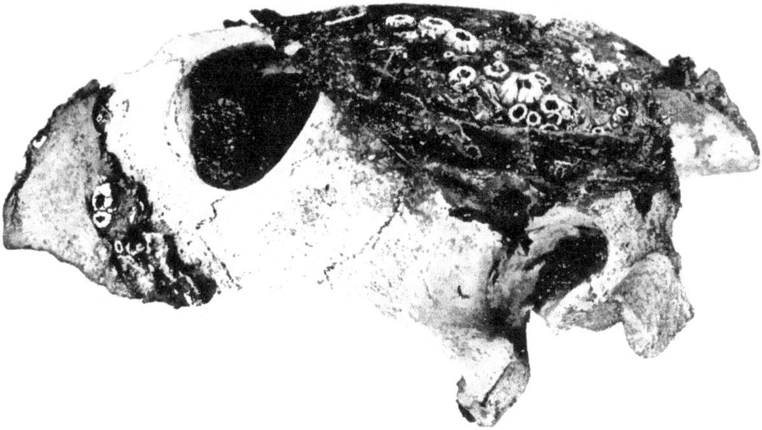

Fig. 35

Platylepas hexastylas Fabricius on skull of Green Turtle

Fig. 36

Coronula diadema Linne

MYSIDACEA

These are small, elongate crustacea usually less than an inch in length. The appendages of the thorax (head region) are branched (biramous)—hence the name Schizopoda (meaning cleft-footed) by which these animals were formerly called. No gills present.

Numerous species are known from our coast, although only one is common in New Jersey.

Mysis americana Smith (Opossum Shrimp)

About half an inch in length, translucent with prominent eyes. Particularly common in winter and early spring on the surface of shallow water, especially in Delaware Bay. These small animals form an important part of the food supply of many of our food fishes.

In this species the eggs are carried in pouches under the thorax, giving the common name "Opossum shrimp."

EUPHAUSIACEA

These shrimp-like crustaceans were formerly grouped with the Mysidacea in the Order Schizopoda because in common with them the thoracic appendages are biramous. However, they differ from the Mysidacea in having gills attached to the thoracic legs. They are considered as of much higher degree of development and are classified nearer the decapod crustaceans.

Meganyctiphanes norvegica Sars

A small shrimp-like form, frequently luminous, that forms an important part of the plankton of the North Atlantic. The only New Jersey records are from a considerable distance off shore. The species may occur at times in the coastal waters of the state.

AMPHIPODA

This group comprises mostly small, and usually laterally compressed crustaceans, covered with a shiny, segmented cuticle. There are usually seven thoracic legs, and seven abdominal appendages. The first three abdominal appendages are the pliopods or sircurmerets, the next three the uropods, and the last the telson, which is sometimes fused with the last abdominal segment. Gills or branchial vesicles are usually present on the inside base of the last six legs. The various appendages are important in the differentiation of the various species.

While most species, including all the New Jersey forms, rarely exceed an inch or two in length, there are a few known from the deeper ocean waters that reach a length of about $5\frac{1}{2}$ inches.

A few Amphipods hop about on the sandy beaches, but by far the greater number live in tide pools, the shallow water close to shore, and in the off-shore waters of the ocean.

The following are the most conspicuous species to be found in our region.

PLATE XXIV

1. **Talorchestia longicornis** Say
2. **Talorchestia megalopthalma** Bate
3. **Gammarus locusta** Linne
4. **Orchestia planensis** Kröyer
5. **Orchestia grillus** Bosc
6. **Cerapus tubularis** Say
7. **Caprella auctifrons** Latreille
8. **Ancinus depressus** Say
9. **Cirolina concharum** Stimpson
10. **Livoneca ovalis** Say
11. **Idotea balthica** Pallas
12. **Limnoria lignorum** Rathke

PLATE XXIV.

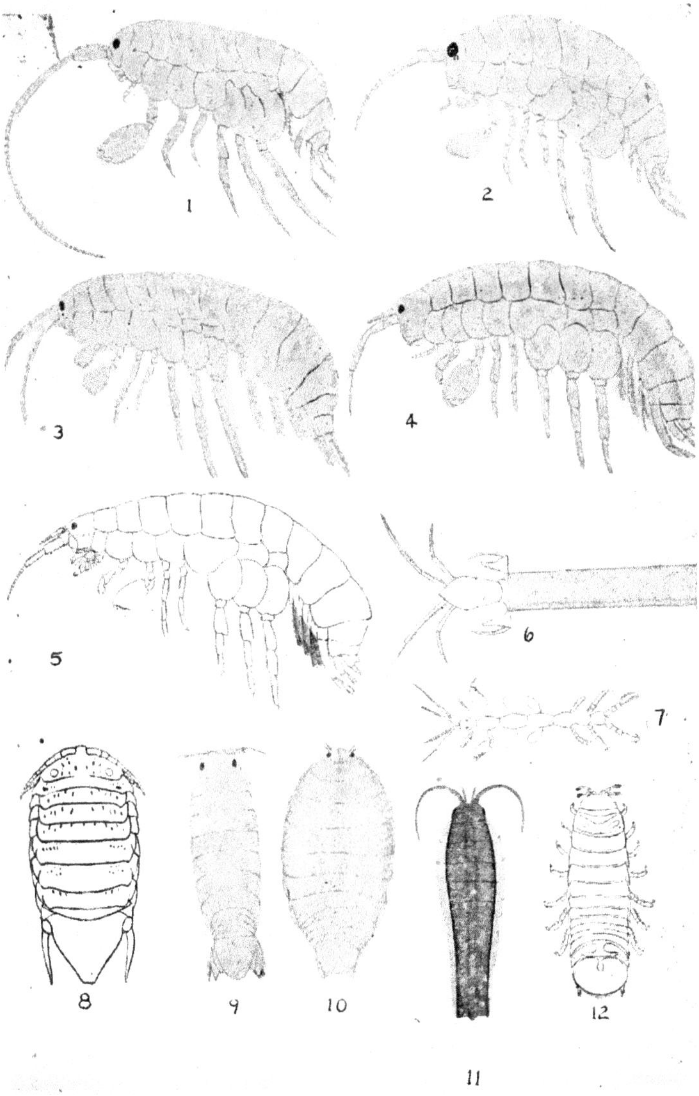

Orchestia platensis Kröyer (Beach Flea)
(O. agilis Smith)

PLATE XXIV. Fig. 4

Small, ½ inch or less in length, light brown in color; occurs in great numbers among moist sea-weed washed on the beach near high water mark; jumps out rapidly when disturbed. Found along the whole coast.

Orchestia grillus Bosc
(O. palustrus Smith)

PLATE XXIV. Fig. 5

Larger than the above (about 1 inch in length), with longer first antennae; light brown in color. Found among grass in salt marshes; does not hop about as much as the above. Cape Cod to Texas.

Talorchestia longicornis Say
(Talitrus longicornis Say)

PLATE XXIV. Fig. 1

Resembles *Orchestia agilis*, except for being whitish in color; about 1 inch in length; long antennae. Lives in small burrows near and above high water mark, usually farther from the water than the home of *O. agilis*; hops about the sand particularly at night. Cape Cod to New Jersey.

Talorchestia megalopthalma Bate
(*Talitrus megalopthalmus Bate*)

PLATE XXIV. Fig. 2

Similar in habits to the above; distinguished by its shorter antennae and very large eyes; not nearly as common. Maine to New Jersey.

Gammarus locusta Linne (Scud)

PLATE XXIV. Fig. 3

Resembles the beach fleas in general appearance but is usually larger and lives exclusively in water; very common among seaweed, under stones, etc., in shallow water. Arctic to Virginia and probably southward.

Cerapus tubularis Say (Tube Scud; Tube Shrimp)

PLATE XXIV. Fig. 6

This animal lives in a small tube which it carries about with it. Often very abundant in New Jersey coastal waters.

Caprella auctifrons Latreille (Skeleton Shrimp)
(*C. geometrica Say*)

PLATE XXIV. Fig. 7

Very slender; walks like the measuring worm. Common on oyster shells in Delaware Bay and in shallow water in general throughout the state.

ISOPODA

Isopods differ from Amphipods in that their bodies are flattened dorso-ventrally instead of laterally. In other words, they are flattened on top and bottom. The two groups resemble each other in size and in many details of anatomy. As in the Amphipods there are 6 or 7 pairs of legs.

Some species of Isopoda may be found among seaweed, under rocks or among woodwork in the intertidal zone, while others swim in the sea either on the surface or at considerable depths. A large number of species are parasitic.

The following are the most frequently encountered species of this region.

Idotea balthica Pallas
(I. marina Linne)

PLATE XXIV. Fig. 11

The commonest New Jersey isopod; a greenish form about 1 inch long; exceedingly abundant in tide pools and among seaweed in shallow water. It has also been found on the surface of the ocean many miles off shore. Common from Delaware northward; local farther south.

Livoneca ovalis Say (Sea Louse)

PLATE XXIV. Fig. 10

Parasitic on the gills of numerous fish caught along the New Jersey coast.

Cirolina concharum Stimpson

PLATE XXIV. Fig. 9

Very common in New Jersey waters in winter: free swimming or parasitic.

Limnoria lignorum Rathke (Gribble)

PLATE XXIV. Fig. 12

A small form, 1/5 inch in length that bores into wood doing considerable damage to piling, etc. The animal is covered with minute hairs. In New Jersey it is present from low water mark to about 10 fathoms, more frequent near shore.

Ancinus depressus Say

PLATE XXIV. Fig. 8

This species was originally described from Egg Harbor (Bay) by Thomas Say in 1818. It was not collected again until very recently. It is now known to be common along the New Jersey and Delaware coasts and probably occurs elsewhere along the Atlantic seaboard.

STOMATOPODA

These animals are elongate and somewhat resemble the lobster, although the abdomen is longer in proportion and the legs are very different. Because of their peculiarly formed chelipeds, or great claws, which resemble those of the praying mantis of our gardens, they are commonly called mantis shrimp. The carapace or shell is softer and does not cover the entire thorax (head and neck region). The gills are on the abdominal appendages. Only one species is known from New Jersey. A few closely related forms are known from more southern waters.

Fig. 37

Chloridella empusa Say

Chloridella empusa Say (Squill; Mantis Shrimp)
(*Squilla empusa Say*)

Fig. 37

This stomatopod is rarely seen in New Jersey waters during the summer, but sometimes is very conspicuous during October and November in shallow water or stranded on the beach, particularly in the southern part of the state. It is horny, brown in color, and from 8 to 10 inches in length. Known from Cape Cod to Florida, especially in muddy association.

DECAPODS

(Crabs, Shrimp, Lobsters, etc.)

The decapods are the most conspicuous group of Crustacea. To this group belong the crabs, lobsters, shrimp and other related forms. When adult there are five pairs of legs of which the first pair, in crabs at least, forms conspicuous claws or chelae. (The name decapoda means ten legs.) The head and thorax (neck region) are united into a cephalothorax which is covered by a chitinous or calcareous shell or carapace. The eyes are on stalks.

Many decapods are of economic importance because of their food value. Shrimp, lobsters and crabs are gathered for the market along the Eastern seaboard. The Spiny Lobster (*Palinurus argus*) is found along the Florida coast and is equally delicious as the nothern lobster (*Homarus americanus*). Crawfish, inhabitants of fresh and brackish water are also frequently eaten, especially in the South. In Cuba they are known as "langustina" and are considered a delicacy.

The following is the current classification of the Decapoda:

Natantia

Usually with well developed abdomen and compressed cephalothorax. Shrimp.

Reptantia

Lobster and crab-like forms; divided into four groups:

1. *Palinura*: Abdomen extended; rostrum short or wanting; cheliped (large claw) absent. Not represented in this region—Spiny Lobster.
2. *Astacura*: Abdomen extended; rostrum short; cheliped present. Lobster.
3. *Anomura*: Abdomen usually bent under cephalothorax or more or less spirally twisted and concealed in a shell; last pair of thorasic legs reduced in size and extended upwards. Hermit Crabs, Hippa, etc.
4. *Brachyura*: Abdomen shorter than cephalothorax and permanently folded under it; no uropod (tail fin). True Crabs.

According to older classification the two divisions were Macrura and Brachyura—the former including the shrimp, lobsters, hermit crabs and the like, while the latter included the true crabs. The term Macrura is not used today while the term Brachyura is still used for the crabs but is a subdivision of Reptantia.

Natantia

(True Shrimp)

Crago septemspinosus Say (Shrimp)
(*Crago vulgaris Verrill*)

Fig. 39

The common shrimp of the New Jersey coast. It occurs in great numbers in shallow water from

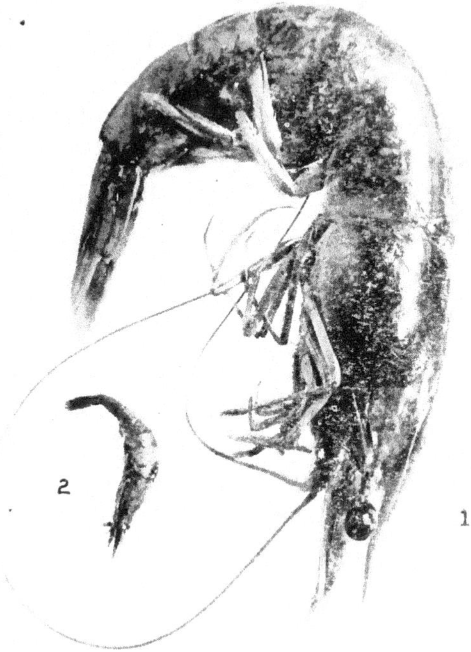

Fig. 39

(1) **Penaeus setiferus** Linne (2) **Crago septemspinosus** Say

Labrador to South Carolina. Usually pale in color, occasionally speckled or gray. This shrimp rarely exceeds $2\frac{1}{2}$ inches in length and is too small to be used to any extent as food by man although it is devoured by fish and other sea animals.

Fig. 38

Palaemonetes vulgaris Say

Palaemonetes vulgaris Say (Prawn; Shrimp)

Fig. 38

Usually slightly smaller than *Crago* and more translucent and almost colorless. It differs from *Crago* also by its longer rostrum and by having its first two pairs of legs chelate (equipped with forcep-like pincers) whereas in *Crago* the first pair is very stout and subchelate. An inhabitant of brackish water and muddy associations rather than the open ocean with *Crago*. Known from Massachusetts to Florida and along the Gulf Coast.

Palaemontes carolinus Stimpson

Occurs with the above but very much rarer. This species is exceedingly difficult to distinguish from *P. vulgaris* and has the same distribution. The following key from Kemp [1] will help the student differentiate these two species:

Outer antennular flagellum with free part of shorter ramus very little longer than fused part.

1. Records of Indian Museum, vol. 27, pt. 4, p. 317.

1 tooth on carapace behind orbit; carpus of second leg longer than palm and half fingers ......*carolinus.*

Outer antennular flagellum with free part of shorter ramus 1½ times as long as fused part; 2 teeth generally present in carapace behind orbit; carpus of second leg not longer than palm in adult female, in male not longer than palm and 1/3 of fingers ....*vulgaris.*

Penaeus setiferus Linne (Southern Shrimp)

Fig. 39

This is the common shrimp of southern waters and is highly valued as food. Although it does not not occur in commercial numbers north of Chesapeake Bay, it is occasionally found in New Jersey waters. When full grown it normally reaches about 6 inches in length; some abnormally large individuals have been taken from New Jersey waters, one measuring 11 inches.

Penaeus brasiliensis Latreille (Brazilian Shrimp or Prawn)

Differs from the above by having a groove on each side of the ridge which runs through the center and whole length of the carapace. Much rarer than the above and not seen in New Jersey for many years; frequents brackish and fresh water along the southern coast. Of less commercial value because it cannot be shipped in a fresh condition.

Fig. 40
Homarus americanus Milne-Edwards

Reptantia

1. Astacura

Homarus americanus Milne-Edwards (Lobster)

Fig. 40

The common Lobster of the North Atlantic Coast which is known from Labrador to Delaware and locally farther south. In the northern part of New Jersey lobsters are taken near shore, but in the Cape May region they are confined to the colder water farther off shore.

Some years ago lobsters were "planted" on the Rock Pile at Cape May, but none are present there today. They are fairly numerous among the rocks at the Breakwater at Lewes, Delaware.

2. Anomura

Upogebia affinis Say (Mud Lobster)

Light brown in color and somewhat resembling a lobster; integument thin and hairy; lives along muddy shores where it digs burrows near low water mark. Known from Massachusetts southward; not common in New Jersey.

Emerita talpoida Say (Sand Bug; Hippa)
(*Hippa talpoida Say*)

PLATE XXV. Fig. 6

Body egg shaped, white with two conspicuous plume-like antennae which strain the water for micro-organisms which it uses as food.

Very abundant on all sandy beaches of the state. It may be seen burrowing rapidly into the sand, head first, as the waves break upon the beach. Often hundreds of these little Sand Bugs may be seen in tide pools. In late summer and early fall young Hippas are very numerous. Known from Cape Cod to Florida.

Pagarus longicarpus Say (Small Hermit Crab)

This crustacean differs from those we have just seen in that its hind end or abdomen is not protected with a hard covering. It, therefore, must find some means of defending itself from any enemy that might attack its soft and defenceless abdomen, so it steals

PLATE XXV

1. **Cancer irroratus** Say
2. **Ovalipes ocellatus** Herbst
3. **Planes minutus** Linne
4. **Calappa flammea** Herbst
5. **Persephona punctata** Linne
6. **Emerita talpoida** Say
7. **Pinnixia chaetopterana** Stimpson
8. **Pinnotheres ostreum** Say
9. **Pagurus pollicaris** Stimpson
10. " " "
11. **Sesarma reticulatum** Say

PLATE XXV.

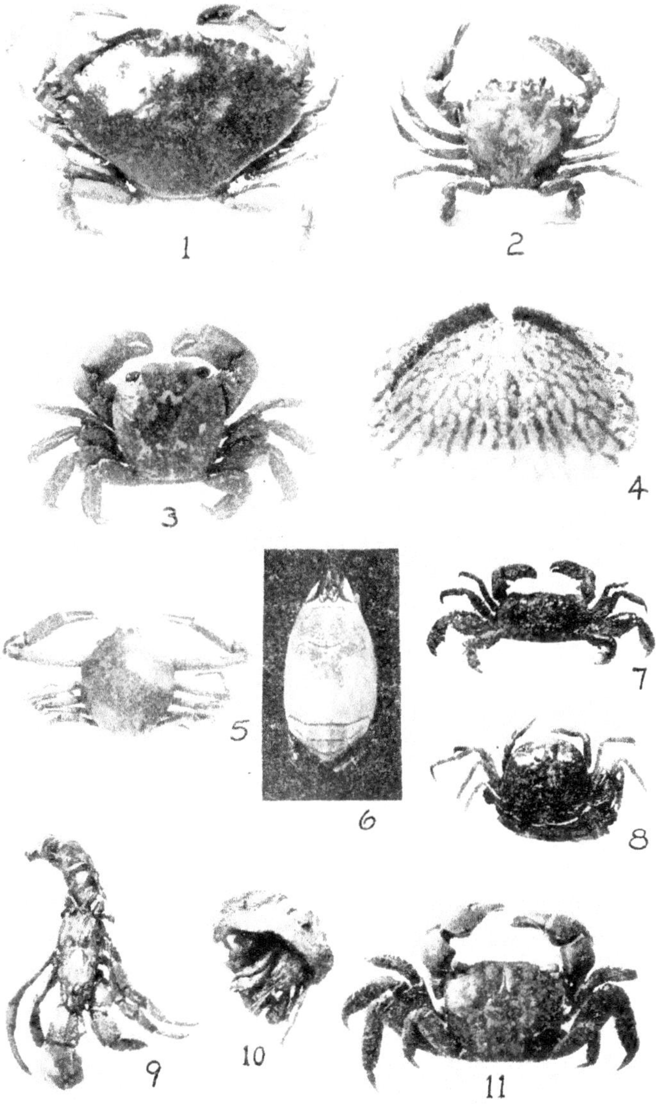

the shell of a sea snail and inserts its abdomen therein. These hermit crabs move about very rapidly, carrying their "houses" on their backs.

As the hermit grows, his house becomes too small for him, and it is necessary for him to seek a new one. The hermit often encounters trouble in this home-seeking task, for two crabs may choose the same house; as a consequence, there is a fight and the victor takes the house while the loser is forced to continue his search elsewhere. At times a homeless hermit crab may attack and dispossess another crab which happens to have a desirable home.

These crabs are very abundant on the bottom of the ocean off the New Jersey coast; they are also frequently found in tide pools along the beach. It is amusing to collect some and watch their antics in a small glass dish or aquarium.

This species usually inhabits shells of *Nassa, Urosalpinx, Eupleura* or other small gastropods. The shells are frequently covered with the hydroid *Hydractinia echinata.*

Very common Massachusetts to Florida.

Pagurus pollicaris Say (Big Hermit Crab)

PLATE XXV. Fig. 9, 10

Larger than the above and with broader hands; usually bright in color and covered with hairs. Inhabits shells of *Fulgur* and *Polinices.* Common with the above, but more apt to be found off shore, although frequently found stranded on the beach. Like the above they are often covered with *Hydractinia.* Common from Massachusetts to Florida.

3. Brachyura

Libinia emarginata Leach (Spider Crab; Sea Spider)

PLATE XXVI. Fig. 2

The common Spider Crab of the New Jersey coast; very common on sandy and muddy grounds from shallow water to 25 fathoms, rarely deeper; found in bays and inlets as well as in the open ocean. The carapace of the Spider Crab is often covered with hydroids, sponges or algae which serve to mask the crab and make it invisible to its enemies. The median line of the carapace has about nine spines. Known from Maine to Florida. Of no commercial value. Sometimes reaches a foot or more in size, usually smaller.

Different from the Blue Crab (*Callinectes sapidus*) in that the claws of this crab are not at all sharp and one may pick it up without danger.

The Spider Crab occasionally lives as a commensal within a jelly-fish.

Libinia dubia Milne-Edwards (Spider Crab)

Six median spines instead of nine and with a longer rostrum (beak); similar habits to the above. Not as common.

Hyas coarctataus Leach (Toad Crab)

The affinities of this to the Spider Crabs are obvious, but it strongly resembles a toad. A northern species not seen in New Jersey since Leidy

PLATE XXVI

1. **Callinectes sapidus** Rathbun
2. **Libinia emarginata** Leach
3. **Portunus gibbesii** Stimpson
4. **Portunus spinimanus** Latreille
5. **Ocypoda albicans** Bosc
6. **Arenaeus cribarius** Lamarck

PLATE XXVI.

recorded it in 1855; not uncommon along the New England coast.

Calappa flammea Herbst (Box Crab)

PLATE XXV. Fig. 4

A buff or light purple crab of southern distribution which is fairly common from Cape Hatteras to Florida. The larval stages occasionally drift as far north as New Jersey or southern New England. Rarely, one survives a mild winter and is found, as an adult, at one of the Jersey beaches. Seen at Corsons Inlet and Cape May Point, New Jersey.

Neopanope texana sayi Smith (Southern Mud Crab)

PLATE XXVII. Fig. 1

Carapace quite convex with a dentate anterior border; 3/5 as long as broad; usually a dark slaty bluish green.

Very common on the oyster grounds of Delaware Bay and generally distributed in shallow muddy water throughout the state. Massachusetts to Florida.

Eurypanopeus depressus Smith (Flat Mud Crab)

PLATE XXVII. Fig. 3

Similar to the above with a flatter carapace. In similar localities to the above but less common: Cape Cod to Gulf of Mexico.

Eupanopeus herbstii Milne-Edwards (Mud Crab)

PLATE XXVII. Fig. 4

Larger than the above two species (up to 2 inches); carapace with a dentate anterior border and with a tubercle just beneath the first tooth; the larger claw has a tubercle at the base of the movable segment; terminal abdominal segment of the male rounded. Gray with black fingers.

With the above three species but not common; Long Island to Florida, more common south of Virginia.

Rithropanopeus harrisii Gould (Brackish Water Mud Crab)

PLATE XXVII. Fig. 2

Smaller than *E. herbstii* (less than 1 inch); dull brown or gray with fingers pale.

Frequents brackish water and salt marshes; known from Dennis Creek, New Jersey, and Mispillion River, Delaware, and can probably be found in similar habitats elsewhere in the region. Known from Massachusetts to Florida.

Eurytium limosum Say

PLATE XXVII. Fig. 7

Differs from the above four species by being more oval and having a nearly smooth carapace with ridges; bright purple-blue in color. A tropical crab known as far north as New York, but very rare north of South Carolina. Some specimens were obtained many years ago from the New Jersey coast.

PLATE XXVII

1. **Neopanope texana sayi** Smith
2. **Rithropanopeus harrisii** Gould
3. **Eurypanopeus depressus** Smith
4. **Eupanopeus herbstii** Milne-Edwards
5. **Uca pugilator** Bosc
6. **Uca minax** Le Conte
7. **Eurytium limosum** Say
8. **Pinnotheres maculatus** Say

PLATE XXVII.

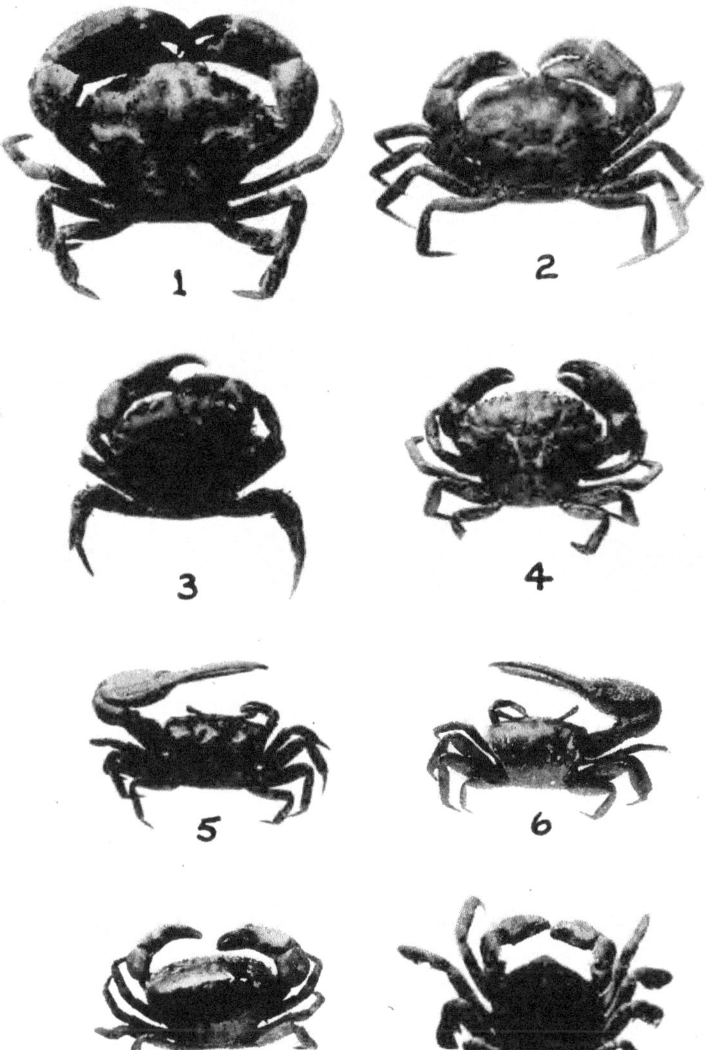

Fig. 41

Carcinides maenas Linne

Carcinides maenas Linne (Green Crab)

Fig. 41

About 2 inches long, slightly wider; characterized by five prominent teeth on each side of the carapace; color greenish with yellow spots above, paler below.

Principally a New England crab living in the rock pools between the tides and in shallow water. The southern limit appears to be South Carolina, but it is rare south of Delaware Bay. In New Jersey it frequents tide pools and shallow water and is usually more common during the colder months.

Callinectes sapidus Rathbun (Blue Crab)

PLATE XXVI. Fig. 1

This crab is probably familiar to everyone because it is very frequently used as food. It lives in muddy regions all along the coast of New Jersey and is particularly abundant in bays and harbors. Summer visitors to the New Jersey often go crabbing from the ends of piers or from row boats in the shallow bays.

It has a hard shell and five pairs of legs. The front pair of legs is larger than the rest and is equipped with nipper-like claws. These are used in defence from enemies and in obtaining food. These claws are very sharp and can inflict an extremely painful wound. The next three pairs of legs are smaller and pointed at the tips and are used for walking along the sea bottom. The fifth pair of legs has rounded paddle-like structures at the ends which are used by the crab as oars or paddles when it swims through the water. As the crab grows, the hard blue shell does not grow with it; in the course of time the shell becomes too tight for the growing crab; so the shell splits, and the crab crawls out with a new soft shell of the proper size upon its body. This crab, which we call a *soft shelled crab*, makes especially delicious food. After a time the soft shell hardens and the story is repeated. This process is called moulting, and is the same thing that happens to a great many insects.

Common from Cape Cod to Florida.

Callinectes ornatus Ordway

Closely resembles *C. sapidus*, but distinguished from it by having six front teeth instead of four.

This crab has not hitherto been reported north of Beaufort, North Carolina. However, the young of this species now frequently occur in small numbers during the summer in southern New Jersey. They may be looked for in the inlets and thoroughfares, although they have also been found in Delaware Bay (to 10 fathoms). No adult specimens have been seen in New Jersey or Beaufort; in New Jersey it never reaches over 2 inches in length. The adults are common from South Carolina to the West Indies and in South America. Its nip is said to be more painful than that of *C. sapidus*.

Arenaeus cribarius Lamarck

PLATE XXVI. Fig. 6

Resembles a young *Callinectes* but easily distinguished from it by its color and design. It is light brown or olive and is thickly covered with small rounded white spots; it rarely reaches a length of more than 2 inches. This is a southern species that is rare north of Virginia. Its home is the deeper water off shore but it is frequently carried to the coastal waters or stranded on the beach. It has been seen as far north as Vineyard Sound, Massachusetts.

Portunus gibbesii Stimpson

PLATE XXVI. Fig. 3

Resembles *Callinectes* but thickly covered with small spherical granules; arms long and slender; color reddish brown with small iridescent areas on the carapace (shell); usually about 2 to 3 inches wide.

Known from Massachusetts to Texas, usually in moderately deep water; very rare in New Jersey.

Portunus spinimanus Latreille

PLATE XXVI. Fig. 4

Resembles *P. gibbesii* but distinguished from it by being narrower and rounder and by the absence of the iridescent patches characteristic of *gibbesii.* Yellow-brown or red-brown in color; usually about 2 to 3 inches wide.

Known from New Jersey to South America; rare and usually in moderately deep water. Specimens dredged in Delaware Bay mark a new northern limit for this species.

Ovalipes ocellatus Herbst (Lady Crab)

PLATE XXV. Fig. 2

Easily recognized by its shape and color; white or cream shell covered with small reddish-brown rings; 2 to 3 inches in width; five teeth on each side with three between the eyes.

Very common on sandy ground from between the tides to 20 fathoms or more. It can often be found at low tide on sandy beaches buried in the sand up to its eyes; here the crab waits for its prey. Having seen something promising, it quickly comes from its hiding place, takes a nip with its very sharp claws, and immediately retreats beneath the sand. Often a bather's toe is the subject of such an attack.

Occasionally used as food in the South; Range: Cape Cod to the Gulf of Mexico.

Cancer irroratus Say (Rock Crab)

PLATE XXV. Fig. 1

Sub-oval, broader than long; average size 3 to 4 inches; carapace smooth with nine blunt teeth on each side. Color yellowish closely spotted with red-brown dots.

Common along the rocky shores of New England from shallow water to about 25 fathoms; fairly common in shallow water along the New Jersey coast, but rare south of Cape Henlopen, Delaware, although reported as far as South Carolina.

Occasionally used as food, but not prized as much as *Callinectes sapidus*.

Cancer borealis Stimpson (Jonah Crab)

Very similar to the above but usually larger and with a rougher carapace with irregular granules; the teeth of the lateral margins have denticulate edges.

Common on the rocky shores of New England in shallow and deep water. Not frequent in New Jersey, although occasionally seen with the more common *C. irroratus*, especially in the northern part of the State. Rare south of New Jersey but found in deep water as far south as Florida.

Pinnotheres ostreum Say (Oyster Crab)

PLATE XXV. Fig. 8

Carapace nearly circular, somewhat membraneous; surface smooth and white; rarely more than ½ inch across the carapace (female). The females live as commensals in the mantle cavity of oysters; the males are very minute and are free swimming.

The females are frequently found in oysters taken from New Jersey waters, and in fact, are eaten with the oysters; the males are seldom seen. Known from Massachusetts to Florida and the West Indies.

Pinnotheres maculatus Say (Mussel Crab)

PLATE XXVII. Fig. 8

Carapace slightly firmer than the above and covered with a hairy growth; females about the size of the above; males smaller than the females, but not as small as the males of *P. ostreum*. Females commensal in the shells of the Mussel (*Mytilus edulis*) or other bivalves; males either free swimming or commensal.

Not as common as the above in New Jersey, although occasionally seen in Mussel shells. Similar range.

Pinnixia chaetopterana Stimpson

PLATE XXV. Fig. 7

Carapace transversely oval; slightly more than twice as wide as long; hairy; length of carapace 5 to 6 mm.; width 12 to 14 mm.; lives commensal in tubes of annelid worms (*Amphitrite ornata* and *Chaetopterus permagmentareus*). Male and female about the same size but the carapace is smoother in the female.

Found from Massachusetts to South America; not uncommon in New Jersey especially in tubes of *Amphitrite*; occasionally taken free swimming.

Sesarma reticulatum Say (Marsh Crab)

PLATE XXV. Fig. 11

Carapace rectangular; usually about 1 inch in width, slightly less in length; color dark olive or black.

Lives in holes similar to those of the Fiddler Crab (*Uca*) although of larger size due to the greater size of the crab. Lives near high water mark in mud flats, inlets, etc. Not common in New Jersey although it may occasionally be seen associated with

Uca. It is known from Massachusetts to Florida but is more common south of Virginia.

Persephona punctata Linne (Purse Crab)

PLATE XXV. Fig. 5

An odd-looking crab with a globular carapace thickly covered with granules; legs also with numerous granules; gray-brown; carapace about 1 to 1½ inches in length, the same in width. A southern species, common from Cape Hatteras southward. One specimen was taken from the New Jersey coast 10 miles southeast of Barnegat Light.

Planes minutus Linne (Gulf Weed Crab)

PLATE XXV. Fig. 3

Carapace rectangular, about as wide as long; usually smaller than *Sesarma* and easily recognized by its more brilliant color which is extremely variable. It is usually olive green blotched with light greenish yellow or pale purple and with three small white spots on the front of the carapace.

This is a pelagic crab that lives on floating Gulf Weed (*Sargassum filipendulum*) throughout the whole length of the Gulf Stream. It has been carried at least twice to the New Jersey shore. H. L. Viereck found it at Cape May on September 20, 1904 (Fowler) and the writer found it at Cape May Point on September 24, 1928, after the "Florida-Porto Rico Hurricane." It may be looked for after any severe storm.

Uca pugnax Smith (Marsh Fiddler Crab)

This odd looking crab is often found in great numbers scurrying about the mud flats. The males all have one claw very much enlarged; this large claw is used for fighting and in defending the females. The females have smaller claws of equal size. Fiddler crabs live in burrows in the mud just beyond the reach of the tide; upon the approach of danger they quickly disappear within their holes. The resemblance of the large claws of the male to a fiddle gives the name fiddler crab. Cape Cod to Florida.

Uca pugilator Bosc (Sand Fiddler Crab)

PLATE XXVII. Fig. 5

Similar to the above except that the inner surface of the large claw (cheliped) does not have the oblique ridge which is present in *U. pugnax*. Its color also is different, the carapace being purplish gray with irregular markings of brown, dark gray or violet.

It is usually found in more sandy associations than *U. pugnax*, but is often seen associated with it. Habits and distribution similar to the above; not quite as common in New Jersey.

Uca minax LeConte (Red Jointed Fiddler Crab)

PLATE XXVII. Fig. 6

Larger than the other Fiddlers and easily distinguished by the red marks at the joints of the chelipeds (legs).

It is found in marshes in brackish or almost fresh water. It digs holes, often as big as 2 inches in diameter, considerably above high tide line; it often builds an archway over the mouth of its burrow, which it uses as an "outlook."

Common in the Delaware Bay region in Dennis Creek, Maurice River, etc., and in similar situations elsewhere in the state; known from Cape Cod to Florida.

Ocypoda albicans Bosc (Sand Crab; Ghost Crab)
(*O. arenaria Say*)

PLATE XXVI. Fig. 5

Somewhat resembles *Uca* but without the greatly enlarged claw. Carapace almost square in shape and about 2 inches long; white or gray in color.

This species burrows round holes in the sand near and not infrequently above high water mark. The animals may be seen scurrying very rapidly over the sand and disappearing into their burrows. These holes may be as much as 3 feet deep and often honeycomb the sand with underground passages. The movable eyestalks of these crabs are very conspicuous.

Very difficult to catch because of their great speed. However, because of their nocturnal habits they may often be blinded by a flashlight and thus obtained at night.

From Long Island to South America. They are particularly large and abundant along the North Carolina coast and may often be seen far from the water and even in the sandy streets of some of the towns of the outer beaches of this region. They are often abundant in New Jersey, particularly in the southern part of the state. Young individuals are often conspicuous in the late summer.

CHAPTER THIRTEEN

ARACHNOIDEA

1. XIPHOSURA (King Crabs)
2. PYCNOGONIDA (Sea Spiders)
3. ARACHNIDA (Spiders)

(Not marine—omitted in this book)

XIPHOSURA
(King Crabs)

Although frequently grouped with the Crustacea, the Xiphosura are probably more closely related to the Arachnida (Spiders), although perhaps they should better be placed in a group by themselves.

The Xiphosura form a group of great geological antiquity, closely related to the Trilobites, which lived in the seas of Palaeozoic times, millions of years ago.

Limulus polyphemus Linne (King Crab; Horseshoe Crab)

Fig. 42, 43

This conspicuous animal is found all along the coast from Maine to the Gulf of Mexico. It prefers sandy and muddy associations in bays and harbors where the salinity is not as high as in the open ocean.

Fig. 42
Limulus polyphemus Linne
Cape May, N. J.

Fig. 43
Mating of **Limulus**
St. Petersburg, Fla.

The body of the King Crab is in three parts—a horseshoe shaped head, an approximately triangular abdomen and a spinelike tail. The total length from head to tip of tail may be as much as two feet.

King Crabs are abundant in Delaware Bay. In May and June they come ashore in great numbers to deposit their eggs on the beach near high tide mark. The crabs come up the beach in pairs, the males being the smaller, riding on the backs of the females. After the eggs are deposited in the sand, the males fertilize them, and then the crabs return to the deeper water of the bay.

A number of years ago *Limulus* was much more abundant than at present. Every year many of these crabs are collected along the New Jersey shore of Delaware Bay. They are allowed to dry on the beach in large pens and then are ground up and used as fertilizer. Because of this industry *Limulus* is dying out in some places.

PYCNOGONIDA
(Sea Spiders)

This is another group of uncertain relationship, although it is probably somewhat related to the Arachnida (Spiders). The Sea Spiders(not to be confused with the Spider Crabs) are small creatures with very conspicuous legs. They may frequently be seen among hydroids, seaweeds, submerged logs, etc. Undoubtedly various species are represented in our waters. The following species is the only one actually noted in the coastal waters of New Jersey.

Tanystylum orbiculare Wilson (Sea Spider)
A small spider-like animal, about 1½ mm. long; occasionally found among hydroids, algae or submerged timber. Vineyard Sound to Virginia. Known from Delaware Bay.

CHAPTER FOURTEEN

INSECTA

(Insects)

Insects are not usually regarded as marine, yet there are a few that are so characteristic of the seashore that they merit inclusion here. Of the marine insects, even in a broad sense of the word, the number of species in this region is very small. One of these few, a minute blue collembolan or Spring Tail (*Anurida maritima* Guerin) is occasionally seen among rocks or pebbles in tide pools along the New England and New Jersey coasts. A few closely related species have been found on Long Island beaches but have not yet been found in New Jersey.

The larvae of certain midges (Chironomidae) frequently live in tide-pools feeding on the green algae. These are truly aquatic larvae, breathing oxygen by means of gill filaments. The adults of these midges usually inhabit the region adjacent to the seashore. Occasionally these larvae are dredged at a considerable distance from shore in water up to 20 fathoms in depth. The most common species is *Chironomus oceanicus* Packard, which is known from Maine, Massachusetts and New Jersey and probably lives elsewhere along our coast.

Numerous insects may be considered as maritime since they are to be found in the brackish water of the salt marshes and inlets and yet are not to be found in the open ocean where the salinity is higher. The most conspicuous of these are the larvae of the four species of mosquito—*Aedes sollicitans* Walker, *A. taeniorynchus* Widemann, *A. cantator* Coquillet and *Culex salinarius* Coquillet, which breed only in salt marshes.

Insects are often picked up in a mass of seaweed or other refuse cast up on the beach by the waves. These insects can hardly be considered marine since their presence in the water was probably caused by an unusually venturesome flight which carried them too far for a safe return to land. After a violent off-shore wind the insect drift may be very large. Various groups of insects are represented in this drift. The common Lady Bug is among the most frequent.

The only truly marine insects, in the strictest sense of the word, are a small group of Hemiptera or bugs. Whereas most of the insects mentioned above spend only part of their life (either larval or adult) in the ocean, these hemiptera live their entire life on the surface of the sea. These wholly marine insects belong to a single genus, *Halobates*, of the family Gerridae. All members of this family of insects live on the surface of water either fresh or salt. The familiar Water Spider (*Gerris*) is frequently seen on the surface of our fresh water ponds.

Of the genus *Halobates* about fifteen species have been described. All are inhabitants of tropic and temperate seas. Some have been taken near shore while others are found as much as 400 miles from the nearest land.

CHAPTER FIFTEEN

CHORDATA

The Chordata is the highest phylum of the animal kingdom. It is in this group that all the higher animals are found, even including man. The main characteristic of the phylum is the possession—sometime during life—of a notochord. In higher chordates this notochord becomes surrounded with cartilage or bone and becomes the spinal column. The higher groups of chordates—those that possess a backbone—are the vertebrates and include the fishes, amphibia, reptiles, birds and mammals.

There are a few groups of chordates that do not possess a backbone and therefore are invertebrates and are to be considered in this book. In many of these lower chordates the notochord remains throughout life; in others it disappears after a larval stage.

ENTEROPNEUSTA

Worm-like chordates in which the notochord consist of a hollow dorsal projection of the forward part of the digestive tube.

Dolichoglossus kowalevskyi Agassiz

An elongate worm-like animal made up of three parts, a proboscis, a short neck and a trunk. The trunk is usually orange-yellow, while the proboscis is more pink with the collar a darker tint. It reaches a length of about 6 inches.

It may easily be mistaken for an annelid worm, but may be recognized by its proboscis and neck. It is often common, burrowing into the sand flats between tides from Massachusetts to North Carolina.

TUNICATA

These are degenerate chordates in which the adult is cylindrical or globular and is encased in a cuticular or cellulose covering called the tunic. The most conspicuous tunicates are the Ascidians. Some, the "simple Ascidians", are usually solitary and attached to some solid object. Others, the "Compound Ascidians" are largely colonial forms embedded in a gelatinous substance.

The larval stages are free-swimming and possess a notochord. Later they assume a sedentary habit and undergo considerable changes in structure. In this process of degeneration, the notochord disappears.

Another group, the Thaliecea, comprise the Salpas, pelagic tunicates which are abundant on the surface of most seas.

Thaliacea

Salpa democratica Forskuli (Salpa)

Salpa and related genera pass through an alternation of generations. One stage is solitary and consists of small transparent, ovoid individuals about an inch long, each with two posterior projections. These simple animals reproduce by budding and thus form long chains, the animals always being arranged in two rows. These chains may be a foot or more in length and may be composed of 30 or 40 pairs of Salpas. The individuals of the chain produce eggs and from these eggs new solitary Salpas are formed. Thus the cycle, or alternation of generations is completed. The life history reminds us of that of the hydroids.

Salpa is often very numerous floating on the surface of the sea and may frequently be collected by a tow net or plankton net. Although able to swim with a snake-like motion, Salpa is usually carried by the currents, and thus belongs to the plankton of the sea.

Widespread distribution; often very abundant in summer off the New Jersey and New England coasts.

Simple Ascidians

Molgula manhattensis De Kay (Sea Squirt; Sea Grapes)

Fig. 44

A globular form with two contractile siphons or tubes; often found growing in clusters in shallow

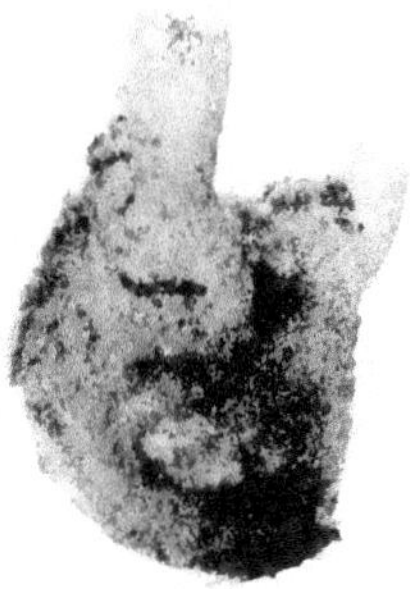

Fig. 44

Molgula manhattensis DeKay

Fig. 45

Botryllus schlosseri Pallas

water attached to piling, sea weed or Eel Grass and often coated with small bits of sea weed, sand, etc.

This species will live throughout the winter unless frozen by the ice; those living in deeper water, where there is little danger of ice, usually reach a larger size. The average size is about an inch in diameter. Its usual color is pale olive green. Maine to North Carolina; often abundant in New Jersey.

Molgula arenata Stimpson

PLATE XXVIII. Fig. 3

Flatter than the above and with shorter siphons; usually heavily coated with sand grains which adhere tightly to the tunic or body. Lives unattached. Found in slightly deeper water than *M. manhattensis* and not nearly as common. Some specimens dredged at McCrie Shoal, 7 miles off Cape May, in 21 feet of water, mark the farthest south that this species has yet been found.

Perophora viridis Verrill

Simple tunicates, about 1/8 inch long, but connected at the base by a common creeping stem; greenish in color. Covers piling, sea weed, etc. in shallow water from Vineyard Sound to Bermuda. Often found in New Jersey's inland waterways. The pulsation of the heart is easily noted under a low powered microscope.

Compound Ascidians

Botryllus schlosseri Pallas

Fig. 45

A colonial form that occurs as fleshy masses attached to algae, eel grass, etc. The individuals of the colony (zooids) form elliptical or stellate patterns with as many as ten individuals in a design. The whole colony is embedded in a common gelatinous tunic. The color of the zooids is variable but usually some bright shade of purple.

Known from New Jersey northward; often completely covers a group of *Molgula*.

Amaroucium pellucidum Leidy

PLATE XXVIII. Fig. 1

A colonial tunicate which forms large gelatinous masses as much as 6 inches in diameter; often coated with sand grains. The individual zooids are elongate and are arranged in tightly crowded stalked

PLATE XXVIII.

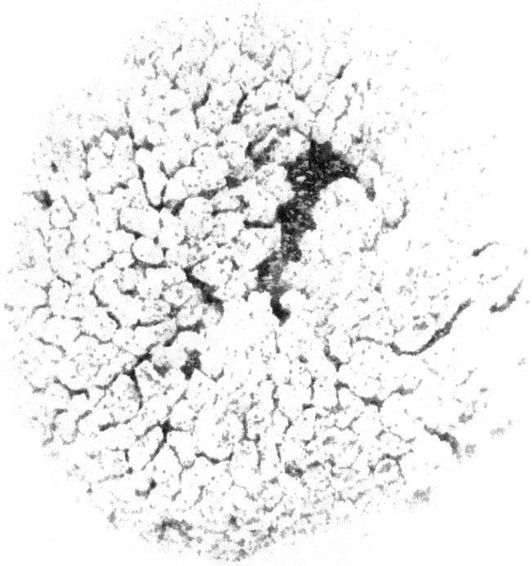

1

2

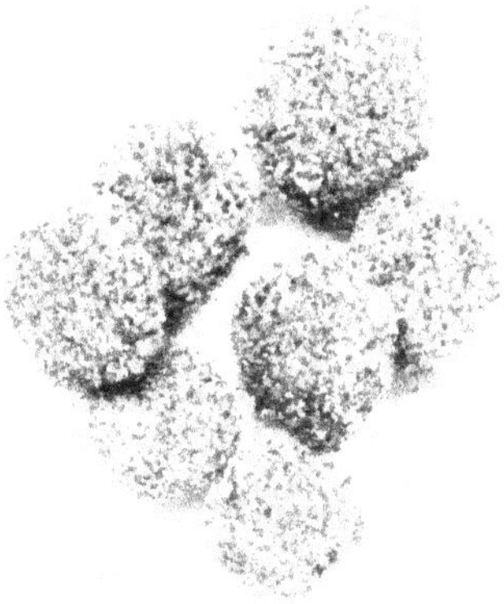

3

1. **Amaroucium pellucidum** Leidy
2. **Amaroucium constellatum** Verrill
3. **Molgula arenata** Stimpson

lobes. Known from Cape Cod to North Carolina, but rare in New Jersey. Characteristic of a sandy bottom.

Amaroucium constellatum Verrill (Sea Pork)

PLATE XXVIII. Fig. 2

Similar to the above but with much larger lobes. The zooids are usually pink or orange and the rest cream. This species is fairly common in rocky associations from Long Island northward. It was recently dredged at the "Old Grounds", 14 miles off Indian River, Delaware. The water was about 130 feet deep and the bottom was rocky.

GLOSSARY OF TECHNICAL TERMS MOST FREQUENTLY USED.

Acontia—Long slender threads equipped with nematocysts or stinging cells, in sea anemones.

Adductor muscle—The muscle used in opening and closing shells of bivalve mollusks.

Algae—Unicellular plants; sea weeds.

Ambulacral groove—The elongate groove on the lower surface of the arms of starfish.

Antennae—Slender hair-like appendages located on the head of various animals; "feelers."

Bivalve—A mollusk composed of two individual valves or shells.

Branchia—A gill.

Byssus—A group of threads secreted by the foot of certain bivalve mollusks for the purpose of attachment.

Carapace—The shell covering the cephalo-thoracic region of crabs and other crustaceans.

Cephalothorax—The body-division of crustaceans formed by the fusion of the head and neck regions.

Cheliped—The pincer or large grasping claw of crabs, lobsters and other crustaceans.

Chetae—Same as setae

Cilia—Small hair-like projections on the outer surface of certain animals; used for locomotion in certain lower forms.

Columella—The axis of a spiral gastropod shell.

Epidermis—The outer layer or skin.

Fascicled—Compound or in bundles.

Gonosome—An individual of a hydroid colony which bears the reproductive organs.

Hydranth—An individual of a hydroid colony which performs the nutritive or digestive functions.

Hydrorhiza—The root-like structure by which the hydroid is attached to stones, shells or other substrata.

Hydrotheca—The chitinous recepticle into which the hydranths of many hydroids may retract.

Hydroid—The sessile, asexual generation of the Hydrozoa.

Lithocyst—A marginal sense organ in certain medusae.

Littoral—Pertaining to the seashore, particularly the intertidal zone.

Madreporic plate—A porous plate on the upper surface of echinoderms through which fluids may enter the system.

Manubrium—The projection of the body of a medusa (jellyfish) which bears the mouth.

Medusa—Jellyfish.

Mesentery—A sheet of leaf-like connective tissue supporting various viscera; in Coelenterates, a partition extending inward from the body wall.

Notochord—A cylindrical rod of cells ventral to the spinal cord and dorsal to the alimentary tract. Occurs in Chordate embryos.

Nematocysts—Stinging cells in Coelenterata.

Operculum—A plate used for closing the shell of gastropod mollusks.

Oriface—Opening.

Osculum—The excurrent opening in sponges.

Parapodium—A flat fleshy segmental appendage found in many marine annelid worms; used for locomotion and respiration.

Pedicellariae—Minute pincer-like organs on the external surface of starfish.

Pelagic—Pertaining to the open sea—not near shore.

Plankton—Animals and plants that drift on the surface of the water; usually without much ability of locomotion.

Planula—The free-swimming, usually pear-shaped ciliated body, into which the egg of a hydroid develops.

Pleistocene—The most recent period of geologic time; frequently spoken of as "The Great Ice Age".

Proboscis—The portion of the hydranth body that usually surmounts the basal tentacles and which contains the mouth. In other animals a tubular extension of any part of the body.

Polyp—An individual member of a hydroid colony.

Rostrum—A projection of the carapace in crustaceans.

Seta—A bristle in worms.

Siphon—A tube-like organ through which water enters and leaves the body of mollusks and ascidians.

Spat—The larval stage of an oyster.

Spicule—A minute calcareous or silicious body in sponges or echinoderms.

Strobila—The attached compound stage in the Scyphozoa.

Tentacle—An elongated tactile organ.

Thorax—The body division of Arthropods following the head; the neck region.

Tube feet—Tubular locomotor organs in echinoderms.

Umbrella—Curved or cup-like body of a jellyfish.

Umbilicus—The depression in gastropod shells at the base of the axis.

Velum—The circular muscular membrane of medusae.

Zooecium—An individual belonging to a bryozoan colony.

Zooid—A member of a hydroid colony.

BIBLIOGRAPHY

The following bibliography makes no pretense at being complete. It merely lists a few books which the reader may consult if he is interested in obtaining further information on the various groups of invertebrate animals found along the East Coast of the United States and especially between Cape Cod and Cape Hatteras. For details on the anatomy of the various animals, the reader is referred to any text book in Invertebrate Zoology

GENERAL

ARNOLD, AUGUSTA F. *The Sea Beach at Ebb Tide.* Century Co., New York, 1901.

BURGESS, THORNTON W. *The Burgess Seashore Book for Children.* Little, Brown & Co., Boston, 1929.

COWLES, R. P. *Biological Study of the Offshore Waters of Chesapeake Bay.* Bull. Bur. of Fish, Vol. 46, 1930

CROWDER, WILLIAM *Dwellers of the Sea and Shore.* Macmillan Co., New York, 1923.

CROWDER, WILLIAM *A Naturalist at the Seashore.* Century Co., New York, 1928.

CROWDER, WILLIAM *Between the Tides* Dodd, Mead & Co., New York, 1931.

HEILPRIN, ANGELO *The Animal Life of Our Seashore.* J. B. Lippincott Co., Philadelphia, 1888.

MAYER, A. G. *Seashore Life.* N. Y. Zoological Society, 1911.

PRATT, H. S. — *A Manual of the Common Invertebrate Animals.* (revised edition). A. C. McClurg & Co., Chicago, 1935.

SHANNON, H. J. — *The Book of the Seashore.* Doubleday, Doran & Co., New York, 1935.

SUMNER, F. B., OSBORN, R. C., COLE, L. J., and DAVIS, B. M. — *A Biological Survey of the Waters of Woods Hole and Vicinity.* Bull. Bur. of Fish., Vol. 31, 1913.

VERRILL, A. E. and SMITH, S. I. — *Report of the Invertebrate Animals of the Vineyard Sound.* Rept. U. S. Fish. Comm., 1871-2, 1874.

WHITEAVES, J. F. — *Catalogue of the Marine Invertebrata of Canada.* Geol. Surv. of Canada, 1901.

PORIFERA

GEORGE, W. C. and WILSON, H. V. — *Sponges of Beaufort (North Carolina) Harbor and Vicinity.* Bull. Bur. of Fish., Vol. 36, 1919.

COELENTERATA

AGASSIZ, A. — *North American Acalphae.* Illus. Cat. Mus. Comp. Zool. Harvard, No. 2. 1865.

FRASER, C. M. — *Some Hydroids of Beaufort, N. C.* Bull. Bur. of Fish., Vol. 30, 1912.

HARGITT, C. W. — *Medusae of the Woods Hole Region.* Bull. Bur. of Fish., Vol. 24, 1904.

HARGITT, C. W. — *Anthozoa of the Woods Hole Region.* Bull. Bur. of Fish., Vol. 32. 1914.

MAYER, A. G. — *Medusae of the World* (3 vol.) Carn. Int. Wash., Pub. 109, 1910.

NUTTING, C. C. — *Hydroids of the Woods Hole Region.* Bull. U. S. Fish Comm., Vol. 19. 1899.

NUTTING, C. C. — *American Hydroids.* (3 volumes). Special Bull. U. S. Nat. Mus., Washington, D. C., 1900-1915.

CTENOPHORA

MAYER, A. G. — *Ctenophores of the Atlantic Coast of North America.* Carn. Inst. Pub. 162, 1911.

NELSON, T. C. — *On the Occurrence and Food Habits of Ctenophores in New Jersey Inland Coastal Waters.* Biol. Bull., Vol. 48, pp. 92-111, 1925.

ECHINODERMATA

AGASSIZ, A. — *Revision of the Echini.* Cat. Mus. Comp. Zool., Harvard, No. 7. 1872.

CLARK, H. L. — *The Synaptas of the New England Coast.* U. S. Fish Comm. Bull. for 1899, p. 21-31. 1899.

CLARK, H. L. — *Echinoderms of the Woods Hole Region.* Bull. U. S. Fish Comm., Vol. 22, 1902.

COE, W. R. — *Echinoderms of Connecticut.*
Conn. Geol. & Nat. Hist. Surv., Bull. 19, Hartford, 1912.

BRYOZOA

BASSLER, R. S. — *The Bryozoa or Moss Animals.*
Smithsonian Rept. for 1920 (Pub. 2633), 1922.

OSBURN, R. C. — *The Bryozoa of the Woods Hole Region.*
Bull. Bur. of Fish., Vol. 30, 1912.

OSBURN, R. C. — *The Bryozoa of the Mount Desert Region.*
Publ. Biol. Surv. Mt. Desert Region, 1933.

VERMES

GEROULD, J. H. — *The Sipunculids of the Eastern Coast of North America.*
Proc. U. S. Nat. Mus., Vol. 44, 1913.

VERRILL, A. E. — *New England Annelids.*
Trans. Conn. Acad., Vol. 4, 1881.

VERRILL, A. E. — *Marine Nemerteans of New England and Adjacent Waters.*
Trans. Conn. Acad. Vol. 8, 1892.

WEBSTER, H. E. — *Annelida Chaetopoda of New Jersey.*
22nd. Rept. N. Y. State Mus. Nat. Hist., 1879.

MOLLUSCA

ALDRICH, BERTHA and SNYDER, ETHEL — *Florida Sea Shells.*
Houghton Mifflin Co., Boston, 1936.

DALL, W. H. — *A Preliminary Catalogue of the Shell-bearing marine mollusks and brachiopods of the South-eastern coast of the United States.* Bull. U. S. Nat. Mus. No. 37. 1889.

DE KAY, J. E. — *Mollusca and Crustacea of New York.* Nat. Hist. of N. Y., 1843.

JOHNSON, C. W. — *List of Marine Mollusca of the Atlantic Coast from Labrador to Texas.* Proc. Boston Soc. Nat. Hist., Vol. 40, No. 1, 1934.

GOULD, A. A. — *Report on the Invertebrata of Massachusetts* (edited by W. G. Binney). Wright & Potter, Boston, 1870.

PROCTER, WILLIAM — *The Molluscs of the Mount Desert Region.* Publ. Biol. Surv. Mt. Desert Region, 1933.

ROGERS, JULIA — *The Shell Book.* Doubleday, Page & Co., 1931.

SMITH, MAXWELL — *East Coast Marine Shells.* Edwards Bros., Ann Arbor, Mich., 1937.

WEBB, WALTER — *Handbook for Shell Collectors* Rochester, N. Y., 1936.

CRUSTACEA

DE KAY, J. E. — *Mollusca and Crustacea of New York.* Nat. Hist. of N. Y., 1843.

FOWLER, H. W. — *The Crustacea of New Jersey.* Rept. N. J. State Museum for 1911, 1912.

HAY, W. P. and SHORE, C. A. — *The Decapod Crustaceans of Beaufort, North Carolina and Surrounding Region.* Bul. Bur. of Fish. Vol. 35, 1918.

HOLMES, S. J. — *The Amphipoda of Southern New England.* Bull. Bur. of Fish. Vol. 24, 1905.

PAULMIER, F. C. — *Higher Crustacea of New York City.* N. Y. State Mus. Bull. 91, 1905.

PILSBRY, H. A. — *The Sessile Barnacles.* Bull. 93, U. S. Nat. Mus., 1916.

RATHBUN, M. J. — *The Grapsoid Crabs of America.* Bull. 97, U. S. Nat. Mus., 1917.

RATHBUN, M. J. — *The Spider Crabs of America.* Bull. 129, U. S. Nat. Mus., 1925.

RATHBUN, M. J. — *The Cancroid Crabs of America.* Bull. 152, U. S. Nat. Mus., 1930.

RATHBUN, M. J. — *The Oxystomatous and Allied Crabs of America.* Bull. 166. U. S. Nat. Mus., 1937.

RICHARDSON, HARRIET — *Monograph of the Isopods of North America.* Bull. 54, U. S. Nat. Mus., 1905.

ARACHNOIDEA

FOWLER, H. W. — *The King Crab Fisheries in Delaware Bay.* Rept. N. J. State Mus. for 1907, pp. 111-119, 1908.

CHORDATA

VAN NAME, W. *Compound Ascidians of the Coasts of New England and Neighboring British Provinces.* Proc. Boston Soc. Nat. Hist., Vol. 34, pp. 339-424, 1910.

VAN NAME, W. *Simple Ascidians of the Coasts of New England and Neighboring British Provinces.* Proc. Boston Soc. Nat. Hist., Vol. 34, pp. 439-619, 1912.

INDEX

Names in italics represent synonyms; words in capital letters represent common names.

C

D

R

S

Milton Keynes UK
Ingram Content Group UK Ltd.
UKHW012034161123
432711UK00006B/407

9 789354 018572